GOSPEL OVERTURES

Gospel Overtures

The Message of the Christmas Stories
in Matthew and Luke

NOEL COOPER

WIPF *&* STOCK · Eugene, Oregon

GOSPEL OVERTURES
The Message of the Christmas Stories in Matthew and Luke

Wipf & Stock
An Imprint of Wipf and Stock Publishers
199 W. 8th Ave., Suite 3
Eugene, OR 97401

www.wipfandstock.com

ISBN 13: 978-1-62564-477-0

Manufactured in the U.S.A.

For my beloved grandsons:
Thomas, Benjamin, Sam and Henry,
three of whom celebrated their first Christmas in 2012.

They shall name him Emmanuel, which means, "God is with us."

Remember, I am with you always, to the end of the age.

MATTHEW 1:21; 28:20

Contents

A Word to the Wise

Christmas is a charming and memorable season for children, and it is perfectly reasonable for well-informed adults to enjoy cribs, candles, and carols, decorated trees, presents, and family feasts. It is *not* possible, however, to be a well-informed adult believer without adding to the value of the Christmas celebration by searching for the deeper meaning of the gospels, a meaning that is beyond the comprehension of young children. Too many adults have found that the faith they accepted as children is inadequate for their adult needs. Regrettably, some have concluded that believing is only for children; many entrust the religious education of their children to other teachers, and live as citizens of the secular world without the support that faith can offer.

Christianity is primarily a religion for adults; the gospel narratives are intended to inspire adult faith. Searching for the message intended by the authors of the gospels will involve significant effort, and a willingness to learn more about the Hebrew Scriptures and the New Testament. *Gospel Overtures* is intended to help readers appreciate the depth of the gospels, and as a result to grow as believers.

I would be pleased to engage in conversation with readers about the deeper meaning of the Christmas stories, via *nhpcoop@yahoo.ca*.

Noel Cooper
Holy Saturday
The first day of Passover
April 7, 2012

Acknowledgments

This book grew out of a series of Advent talks I was invited to give at a Catholic parish in Toronto in 2011. I offer my sincere thanks to Wayne Debly for proposing this series and for his constructive comments on this text.

After the lecture series was completed, I had presented only half of what had been prepared, so I wrote out what I had said and what I had intended to say, for future reference. I also wish to acknowledge the wisdom and insight gleaned from the audiences at those presentations and from the various sources that are listed in the brief bibliography at the back of this book. I hope that I have complemented those insights, especially in paragraphs that consider "how can this passage be applied to the lives of contemporary believers?"

I also wish to express my thanks to Beverly O'Grady, who commented positively about the manuscript and eventually guided me to Wipf and Stock Publishers, and to Sean McEvenue, a Scripture scholar and retired university professor, who offered detailed and valuable analysis of my ideas.

This manuscript has been presented to and rejected by at least four Catholic publishers, only one of whom even agreed to read the manuscript. The topic is apparently considered very delicate in Roman Catholic circles. I am grateful to Wipf and Stock for agreeing to publish this book, which may be of interest to many believers beyond the Catholic community. I sincerely hope that adult believers will experience in a deeper way the greatness of Jesus as he is presented in the infancy narratives of Matthew and Luke.

Introduction

Gospel Overtures

The gospels according to Matthew and Luke begin with what are known as "the infancy narratives." Each in its own way, those two gospels tell of preparations for the coming of Jesus, his birth, and subsequent events as a result of which some people accept Jesus as God's greatest gift to humanity, and some reject him, usually for reasons related to preserving their own wealth and power.

The gospels should always be understood as proclamations of the faith of the early Christian communities from which they arose, rather than simply as a report of historical events. A primary goal in Scripture study is to understand the meaning that was intended by the author, and to consider to what extent that meaning can support our personal faith journey.

The gospels of Matthew and Luke were written more than fifty years after the death and resurrection of Jesus, and more than eighty years after his birth. The infancy narratives seem to have taken their final form rather late in the process that led to the gospels as we know them, and the earliest versions of those stories may have been written by someone other than the final evangelist. A brief narrative of the development of the New Testament will be found early in the following pages.

The infancy narratives in Matthew and Luke are so different from each other that they are almost incompatible on the level of historical fact. Most contemporary scholars agree that neither of the authors had read the other's account before composing his own narrative of Jesus's conception and birth. Though the gospels often disagree in the area of "historical fact," it is vitally important to realize that the authors were far more interested in theological insight than in the reporting of facts.

On the level of theological reflection, the narratives are quite compatible, as they proclaim the greatness of Jesus and seek to persuade us readers that Jesus and God's kingdom are good news for us, responding to our deepest spiritual yearnings.

It is important to note that the Hebrew Scriptures provided the tradition and the symbolism that formed the basis of the gospels' understanding of the greatness of Jesus. Though the gospels did present Jesus in competition with religious and historical figures of other cultures, almost all the terms used by the evangelists came from the Jewish tradition. We cannot fully understand what the authors intended to convey without exploring the Hebrew Scriptures that they knew so well, and referred to in their narratives.

Themes found in the infancy narratives are restated and reinforced throughout the body of each gospel. As a result, the Christmas stories can be understood as "overtures" to the gospels, in the same way that the music at the beginning of an opera or a musical introduces the themes that will be repeated in the body of the play.[1]

In the following pages, we will present the infancy narratives in the gospels of Matthew and Luke, making an effort to be faithful to each author's theological insight and also searching for the support and the challenges that the gospels offer us as contemporary disciples of Jesus.

1. The word "overture" is the thematic word describing the infancy narratives in Borg and Crossan, *First Christmas*. I am grateful for their insight.

Chapter 1

Background

The New Testament Context

1. JESUS'S MOST IMPORTANT TEACHING

According to at least three of the gospels, the teaching that Jesus considered most important was expressed in his simple and frequent proclamation of what he called good news: "The kingdom of God has come near" (Mark 1:15; Luke 10:9). Jesus devoted most of his teaching to the kingdom of God: many of the parables are introduced with the words "The kingdom of God is like . . ." He also presented his healings as examples of what can happen when the kingdom of God enters a person's life (see Luke 11:20).

The kingdom of God was central to Jesus's proclamation, but unfortunately, the phrase means very little to many modern believers. In truth, it is a credible and attractive teaching that can have a profound effect on our lives.

The reign of God[1] is *God's loving initiative* to make us whole. Jesus's most important teaching was not about what *we* should do

---

1. Many contemporary theologians prefer to use the term "reign" rather than "kingdom," because reign implies the *influence* of God in people's lives, and reduces the political (and masculine) overtones of the word "kingdom."

(for example, "love one another"), but about what God offers to do for us.

The reign of God is very much related to our life on earth. In Luke 17:20–21 Jesus says, "The kingdom of God is among (or within) you." Even the phrase "kingdom of Heaven" refers to life on earth rather than to life after death. In Hebrew understanding, heaven was the home of God and the angels. One professor suggested that we understand the kingdom of Heaven as the spiritual power of God (God's influence, God's grace) that comes from heaven to us.

To repeat, the reign of God is *the action of God in our lives*. Jesus proclaimed repeatedly that God offers to reign in our hearts. If we open our hearts to the influence of God, if we allow God to rule our lives, God will transform us and enable us to grow toward wholeness,[2] to love generously and to be true to ourselves and in that way to be faithful to God. The reign of God is something God does for us. It is not something we accomplish on our own; it is not something we earn; it is God's gift.

The reign of God has a communal implication as well. None of us can open our hearts to the action of God in isolation. No one grows to wholeness alone. The Christian community is composed of believers who have chosen to allow God to rule in their hearts, and who support each other by expressing their faith together, by trying to live as followers of Jesus, and by praying together. We need each other if we are to grow toward wholeness.

The reign of God is good news, since it assures us that we are not expected to grow toward wholeness by our own efforts. As we shape our lives by our decisions, as we seek to be free, happy, loving and fully human, Jesus offers us the power of God's love working within us, leading us to wholeness. God offers us ongoing spiritual support, helping us to be wise as we deal with what life brings us, to make sense of our lives, to know what is the right thing to do, to have the courage to do what we know is right, and to perceive where we belong in the universe with reverence and awe.

2. For a more extensive discussion of "wholeness," please consult my book *What Makes Us Whole*.

The preceding paragraphs have expressed in several ways the meaning of Jesus's teaching about the reign of God. In a different way, they respond to a question that all believers must consider: what can we ask of God? Prayer that asks God to change circumstances miraculously is problematic. Prayer that asks God to support us spiritually as we face the challenging circumstances of our lives is more believable.

What we are invited to do, then, is to accept God's offer: open our lives to the transforming action of God, allow God to reign in our hearts, and cooperate with the grace of God as we make the responsible decisions that shape us as faithful followers of Jesus.

The teaching about the reign of God is central to every gospel, and is the focus of the infancy narratives, the overtures to the gospels of Matthew and Luke. The gospels challenge believers with the fundamental question: will you let God reign in your life?

2. BIBLICAL TRUTH AND HISTORICAL FACT

When the ancient peoples wished to express an important truth, they didn't write history books or philosophy books. Often, they wrote stories. The parables of Jesus are an excellent example. When he was asked, "Who is my neighbor?," he didn't give a conceptual response (such as the definition I learned as a child, "mankind of every description"). Instead, Jesus told a story. When faced with that question, he told the parable of the Good Samaritan (Luke 10:25–37), a memorable example of fiction used to teach a lesson. There was no historical "Good Samaritan"; he is a fictional character whose actions teach us what it means to be a good neighbor. Hearing the statement that the Good Samaritan is a fictional character, students would invariably ask, "So it's not true, right, sir?" My answer always was, "It *is* true; it teaches important truth about God and human values. It's just not a historical fact."

People of the twenty-first century prefer to rely entirely on factual information, and tend to dismiss as "untrue" anything that isn't factual. As a society and as a community of believers, we definitely need greater respect for the truth expressed in literature and poetry, and for the depth and meaningfulness of symbolic writing. The Bible (including the infancy narratives) is less "newspaper report" than "reflection on the place of God in human life," often expressed in poetry, myth, or other forms of symbolic language—a matter of great importance that is far deeper than a presentation of simple facts. What is truly significant is recognizing meaning, getting to know Jesus, believing, and considering the importance of his teaching for our lives.

3. THE DEVELOPMENT OF THE NEW TESTAMENT

The New Testament developed over a period of some eighty years after the death and resurrection of Jesus. For several decades, the narratives were passed by word of mouth from parent to child to grandchild in the context of various communities of believers. The following brief description of the process is told with a specific focus on the gospel accounts of Jesus's birth and childhood.

THE LETTERS OF PAUL

Our earliest written Christian documents are the letters of Paul. Paul never met Jesus, and indeed persecuted the early Christian communities before unexpectedly converting to Christianity within ten years after the death of Jesus. After becoming a disciple, Paul apparently understood the greatness of Jesus better than his good friends, who were mostly illiterate Galilean workers. It was Paul, proud as he was of his Jewish heritage, who understood that Jesus's proclamation of the reign of God was intended for all humanity. The letters that were actually composed by Paul himself were written between the years 49 and 65 of the first century. By the time of Paul's death, no gospel had yet been composed. The traditions that were later put in writing as gospels existed primarily in oral form for more than four decades after the resurrection. Paul knows nothing of what we call the Christmas stories; his only references to the birth of Jesus are found in the Letter to the

Romans 1:3 ("descended from David according to the flesh") and in Galatians 4:4, where he describes Jesus as "born of a woman, born under the law [of Moses]."

The Gospels

The gospels are statements of faith. The first of them, Mark, was likely completed shortly after the year 70 CE.[3] From an early age, everyone should be aware that the accounts of Jesus's life are not like newspaper reports. They aren't biographies or history books: they are *gospels*. That word means "good news." The people who wrote the gospels were convinced that Jesus is good news for us; he provides the answers to the deepest questions of life. The gospels do have a basis in fact: Jesus really lived, and we have some very good information about his life and his teachings. Still, the accounts of his life evolved during the decades of oral transmission before they were written down.[4] Some scholars attempt to discern which details are historically reliable, but the important purpose of learning about the gospels is to get in touch with Jesus and his teaching, rather than to be concerned primarily about historical facts.

The good news of Jesus was transmitted to numerous communities in western Asia and later in Europe by word of mouth for a few decades after his death and resurrection (which took place likely before the year 30 CE). Oral transmission is fundamentally conservative: anyone who has read a book to a child knows that children will not permit variations (like skipping a couple of

3. Modern scholars use CE (for "Common Era") rather than AD (for "Anno Domini," meaning "in the year of our Lord") out of respect for the millions of people in the world who use the same dating system, but who do not consider Jesus to be their Lord.

4. If you have questions about this brief summary of the process that led to the New Testament as we know it, please seek more extensive introductory books about the New Testament. This discussion presents a mainstream contemporary understanding of Scripture; it will not be accepted by literalist or fundamentalist readers. My book *Language of the Heart* provides a popular account; many more scholarly presentations are available.

pages). The "broken telephone" activity often used in classrooms (where a message is whispered to one person, and then is passed to others one by one before it emerges garbled at the end of the string) is exactly the *opposite* of oral transmission, where a whole community receives the story and participates in the retelling of it. When stories evolve as a result of developing insight, the whole community takes part in the process. Secrecy and whispering are not part of the procedure. Still, there is no question that accounts do change as the result of evolving faith.

After more than forty years of oral transmission, the written gospels began to appear. The four that we consider most important developed in four communities that probably had little contact with each other. Each of them presents the greatness of Jesus in its own distinctive way. Today, we cherish the *differences* between the gospels. We respect the way each gospel presents Jesus, like works of art by four different artists reflecting on the same scene or event, or like four spotlights focused on one person from different angles. Each of the gospels illuminates various features of the person of Jesus. Without any one of them, some aspect of the greatness of Jesus would be in darkness.

We know what these four communities believed about Jesus, some forty to seventy years after his death. We can speculate about what really happened forty to seventy years earlier, but the search for "facts" isn't of prime importance.

AUTHORSHIP OF THE GOSPELS

To be honest, most scholars also agree that we don't know the names of *any* of the authors of final form of the gospels, but it is possible that the names in the titles (which were added many years later and were not part of the original manuscripts) have some connection with the tradition that gave us the various gospels. To take one example, it is likely that John, the blustery son of Zebedee (see Mark 4:17) who was presumably a marginally literate fisherman, proclaimed his memories of Jesus in a number of communities in the years after the resurrection. Each of those communities then possessed "the gospel according to John" in oral form. Many decades and a few generations of Christians later, a brilliant faithful literary genius not known to us by name, living in one of those communities, transformed the tradition according to his own theological and symbolic understanding, and composed what we know as the gospel according to John. The son of Zebedee may have originated the tradition in that community, but it is unlikely that he wrote the gospel as we know it.

A similar rationale could be proposed regarding the authors of other gospels. The tax collector who became a follower of Jesus is identified as "Matthew" only in the gospel according to Matthew (9:9). Mark 2:14 and Luke 5:27 know the tax collector as Levi. Lists of Jesus's inner circle of twelve in the Synoptic Gospels[5] all include the name of Matthew without reference to a Levi who had a previous career as a tax collector for the Romans. No doubt the Matthew who is listed among the Twelve went out to preach about Jesus; some fifty years later, likely someone else in one of the communities where Matthew preached transformed the oral tradition into the written document that we have as "the gospel according to Matthew."

Eyewitness status has never been claimed for the authors of Mark and Luke: those names appear nowhere in the accounts of Jesus's ministry. The traditional authors' names are linked (unverifiably) to minor characters in other early Christian writings, but most likely the gospels according to Mark and Luke are based on testimony preserved in early communities, and were transmitted through generations of believers before being composed by authors whose names we likely don't know.

---

5. The gospels according to Matthew, Mark and Luke are so similar to each other that they are grouped under the title "Synoptic" (from the Greek words for "seen together"). Many narratives and teachings of Jesus can easily be compared since they are reported in two or three of the Synoptic Gospels. The Gospel of John is so different that such comparison is almost impossible. For one example, John has no list of "The Twelve."

THE GOSPEL ACCORDING TO MARK

Most scholars agree that the first gospel to be written in the form we have it now was the gospel according to Mark. The earliest gospel was written near the year 70 CE, more than forty years after the death and resurrection of Jesus. The Gospel of Mark has a theological purpose: it is designed to persuade the reader that Jesus is "good news," that he is the fulfillment of Jewish hopes ("Messiah" or "Christ"), and that he is "Son of God" (see Mark 1:1). What we know with historical reliability is what one Christian community believed about Jesus at the time of writing: again, we know what they *believed* then. The effort to discover what really happened forty years before the writing of the gospel is an interesting but uncertain exercise. What Mark's gospel really wants to achieve is to persuade readers to believe in Jesus as the Messiah and the Son of God.

According to Mark, Jesus was a human being who lived at a specific time in a specific culture. He was not some kind of mythical superman who knew everything and could do anything whenever he wanted (see Mark 6:5). He grew up in a small village called Nazareth, and worked all his life, probably in the construction trade. Everyone in his home village thought of him as an ordinary person, except that apparently he never married. None of the townspeople of Nazareth during Jesus's lifetime had ever heard of the accounts of his birth that we know from Matthew and Luke; neither had the community that gave us Mark's gospel.

The preceding paragraph is quite compatible with believing that Jesus is "Son of God." Paradoxically, the Gospel of Mark presents the *death* of Jesus as the moment when he was recognized as Son of God (Mark 15:39).[6] The centurion's cry of belief depends on a profound understanding of God (not historically likely coming from a Roman soldier)—a God perceived by the author not as a worker of supernatural wonders, but as self-giving Love and faithful integrity. Seeing those qualities in the actions of Jesus are what

6. The voice from heaven at Jesus's baptism announces, "You are my beloved Son," but in Mark that proclamation is addressed only to Jesus himself. Not until his death does any human call Jesus "Son of God" in Mark.

inspired Mark to believe that Jesus was somehow the presence of God in our world, living a single human life.[7]

The Gospels according to Matthew and Luke

If you compare Matthew and Luke with Mark, it seems probable that both authors copied many episodes from Mark, verbatim in many cases, and with deliberate adjustments in other instances. Seven-eighths of the text of Mark is found in Matthew and Luke. Each author also presents material that is not in Mark—some found in both Matthew and Luke, other material distinctive to the respective gospels.

Primary among their distinctive additions to Mark are the Christmas stories, which are completely different in the two gospels (Matthew and Luke). Most scholars speculate that Matthew was written in the early 80s of the first century, and Luke was written some time after the year 90. The details and purposes of their well-known narratives of the conception, birth and childhood of Jesus will comprise the rest of this book.

The Gospel according to John

The gospel according to John, the last to be written, has very little in common with the first three gospels. Very few of the incidents reported in John were previously reported in Matthew, Mark and Luke.[8] In John, Jesus's language and style of talking are so differ-

---

7. Please note that Mark's belief in Jesus as Son of God is not related to Matthew and Luke's presentation of the virginal conception of Jesus (unknown to Mark's community). In Mark's gospel Jesus is perceived as Son of God not because of how he was conceived, but because of the way he lived and died with self-giving love and integrity, revealing his intimate connection to God.

8. The Gospel of John is so unlike the other three that there was serious debate whether to include it in the New Testament. Several other gospels (Gospel of Thomas, Gospel of Peter, Gospel of Mary Magdalene) were not included, but they are studied today as testimony to what was believed about Jesus in other early Christian communities. Like the favored four gospels, all are pseudonymous.

ent from the sayings in the Synoptic Gospels that most observers believe they present the ideas of Jesus in language developed by the author—his work is a credible interpretation, but not by any means a simple reporting of events or teachings.

The Gospel of John introduces an unprecedented factor into the Christian understanding of the greatness of Jesus—the idea that "the Word of God" existed before Jesus was conceived in Mary's womb. Paul had asserted that Jesus "was declared to be Son of God... by resurrection from the dead" (Rom 1:4); Mark reported that Jesus was proclaimed as Son of God by a voice from heaven that spoke only to Jesus at his baptism (Mark 1:11), and was recognized as Son of God by a Roman centurion at his death (Mark 15:39). Matthew and Luke used their infancy narratives to proclaim that Jesus was Son of God by the power of the Holy Spirit from the beginning of his life in Mary's womb.

The Gospel of John's concept of preexistence had never been imagined by the communities that gave us the first three gospels. John speaks of the Word of God, using a term that had not previously been applied to Jesus; a "word" sums up a reality and expresses it. Opening his gospel with the same phrase that begins the book of Genesis, the author of John claims that Jesus's relationship to God goes back to creation: "*In the beginning* was the Word... All things came into being through him... And the Word became flesh and lived among us" (John 1:1, 2, 14, emphasis added).

Our familiar language about Jesus "coming down from heaven," with its associated de-emphasis of Mark's portrayal of the gritty humanity of Jesus, can be attributed to this insight of John which was unknown to the writers of the Synoptic Gospels.

The Gospel of John has no knowledge of or reference to the infancy narratives as they are presented in Matthew and Luke.

Chapter 2

The Christmas Stories in Matthew

1. INTRODUCTION

In addition to his own personal faith and insight, the author of Matthew apparently used a number of written documents as sources for his gospel. They included the Gospel of Mark which had been composed some ten years earlier, a collection of sayings of Jesus with no narratives attached (now known as Q), and likely some other written and oral material that was known only to Matthew's community. That community, about fifty years old and possibly located in Syria, included many Christians who were heirs of the Jewish tradition. A significant purpose of Matthew's gospel was to present Jesus as the fulfillment of Jewish hopes, to support that segment of his community in their decision to become followers of Jesus.

Matthew developed his infancy narrative as a prelude or overture to the gospel, setting the stage for themes that would be explored in the body of the work. In creating his Christmas story, he may have used materials previously written by others. It is possible that, like the introductions or overtures to many works, the infancy narratives were composed after the body of the gospel.

As we begin a detailed discussion of Matthew's infancy narratives, try to remove from your consciousness all the details that you remember f rom Luke's gospel. That gospel did not exist when Matthew was written; the author of Matthew apparently knew nothing of census, manger, shepherds and angels. He developed his infancy narrative to prepare for his presentation of the good news of Jesus in a way that would respond to the needs of his community.

The first chapter of the gospel has two components, the genealogy of Jesus and the angel's announcement to Joseph about the origin of the child and the role that Joseph is expected to play in his life. Chapter 2 tells the story of the magi who came from afar to honor the newborn child in Joseph's home in Bethlehem, followed by the family's flight to Egypt to escape the murderous king, the massacre of the male infants in Bethlehem, and the family's migration, not to their original home but to the town of Nazareth in the district of Galilee where Jesus was to grow up and live most of his life.

The above summary represents the extent of Christian reflection on the origins of Jesus, at the time of its composition. Remember that none of his townspeople, nor the disciples who followed Jesus during his ministry, nor Paul, nor the author of Mark had ever heard these accounts.

2. MATTHEW'S USE OF PROPHECY (E.G., MATT 2:15)

Before beginning with the first segment of Matthew's gospel, we should look at one of the important techniques Matthew used to support the faith of Christians of Jewish heritage who formed a major part of his community. The author frequently introduces a quotation from the Hebrew Scriptures with a formula like "This was to fulfill what had been spoken by the Lord through the prophet." An interesting and familiar example follows from Matthew chapter 2:

> Now after they had left, an angel of the Lord appeared to
> Joseph in a dream and said, "Get up, take the child and
> his mother, and flee to Egypt, and remain there until I tell
> you; for Herod is about to search for the child, to destroy
> him." Then Joseph got up, took the child and his mother
> by night, and went to Egypt, and remained there until the
> death of Herod. This was to fulfill what had been spoken
> by the Lord through the prophet, "Out of Egypt I have
> called my son." (Matt 2:13–15)

You will have noticed that at the end of the narrative about
the family's flight to Egypt, the gospel writer presents a quotation
from "the prophet": "Out of Egypt I have called my son." Eight
times in the course of the narrative about the beginning of Jesus's
life, the Gospel of Matthew uses a phrase similar to "This was to
fulfill what had been spoken by the Lord through the prophet."

To understand Matthew's use of prophecy, and to experience
the depth and riches of the gospel, we should explore the meaning
of the quotation *in its original context* in the book of the prophet
Hosea before we consider Matthew's fulfillment saying.

The book of the prophet Hosea was written in the eighth century BCE (the 700s). After the death of King Solomon in 930 BCE,
ten of the twelve tribes had seceded from the union rather than be
ruled by any son of Solomon, or any heir of the royal family of King
David. Thus began what is known as the northern kingdom. One
of the issues that caused the secession was that Solomon had con-
scripted every male into his army at puberty, and turned the young
soldiers into slaves to build palaces and stables—and the temple in
Jerusalem—for the king's benefit. Many of those young men who
didn't die while slaving in the king's service were returned to their
families with broken bodies and spirits. Such royal arrogance had
provoked hatred of the king by many families in his realm.

After the division of the nation in 930 BCE, the northern
kingdom (which called itself "Israel") constructed a new capital
city, Samaria. The new nation began its own royal family (pur-
posely *not* "the family of David"), and continued to follow the
religion of Moses at its own new temple. The now-tiny southern

kingdom (called "Judah," composed of only two tribes) retained its allegiance to the royal family of David and continued to worship at the temple built by Solomon in Jerusalem. Both kingdoms were lax in their religious observance; the impression that the northern kingdom was less faithful is the result of the fact that most of the biblical literature originated in the south. The prophet Hosea preached in the northern kingdom, in "Israel."

The passage you are about to read mentions the people of Ephraim. The tribe of Ephraim was thought to be descended from the patriarch Joseph (see Genesis chapters 37–45, popularized some years ago in a musical play about a technicolor dreamcoat). Mary's husband Joseph is linked to the patriarch by this brief quotation in the Gospel of Matthew. The patriarch Joseph was sold into slavery by his brothers, but rose to prominence in Egypt. As well, Joseph in the book of Genesis was renowned for his interpretation of dreams; time after time, Joseph in Matthew's infancy narrative is given instructions in dreams.

First, read Hosea 11:1–9 to experience the prophet's poetic expression of God's heartfelt, steadfast forgiving love for the people. (The excerpts below have been carefully translated in the NRSV version so that they can be read with the image of God as *Mother* in mind. Read the entire passage in your Bible if you prefer.) It is God who speaks in the first person in this passage.

> When Israel was a child, I loved him,
> And out of Egypt I called my son.
> The more I called them,
> The more they went from me . . .
> Yet it was I who taught Ephraim to walk;
> I took them up in my arms . . .
> I was to them like those who lift infants to their cheeks;
> I bent down to them and led them.
> How can I give you up, Ephraim?
> How can I hand you over, O Israel? . . .
> My heart recoils within me;
> My compassion grows warm and tender.
> I will not execute my fierce anger . . .

For I am God; I am no mortal,[9]
The Holy One in your midst,
And I will not come in wrath.

Please read the passage from Hosea two or three times, and reflect on the poet's experience of the forgiving nature of God. Clearly, this beautiful poem expresses God's loving kindness toward a people that was first rescued from Egypt under Moses, then was loved and nurtured by God, but later deserted God and worshipped the gods of their indigenous neighbors. (Baal and "Most High" are named in the passage.) A modern hymn titled simply "Hosea" expresses the central theme of the book of Hosea—God's forgiving love. The hymn's refrain reads:

Long have I waited for your coming home to me
And living deeply our new life.

Perhaps in some way you have strayed like the people of Israel, and need to be reassured about God's forgiving love. The passage from Hosea and the modern hymn may help you to be confident and peaceful.

After you have experienced the meaning of the passage in Hosea 11, it is time to consider the use of that passage in the Gospel of Matthew. The author of the gospel chose a brief phrase from the first verse of that passage, and said it was "fulfilled" in the journey of Joseph's family to Egypt. "I have called my son out of Egypt" (Hos 11:1, Matt 2:15).

People who have been taught to read the Bible literally believe that the prophet predicted that the Messiah would travel to Egypt. Any reasonable reading of the Hosea passage makes it clear that the prophet's original intention had nothing to do with foretelling the future life of the Messiah; it is a poetic and emotional reflection on the history of God's relationship with the people of Israel.

---

9. The New Revised Standard Version uses the word "mortal" as a gender-inclusive translation of the Hebrew word that was formerly rendered in English as "man." The word "mortal" is intended to refer to all of us as human beings, and to contrast God's way of being with ours. I would prefer the term "human."

Matthew's purpose in using that brief quote from Hosea 11:1 was *not* to claim that the prophet literally predicted an event in the Messiah's life. Think of Matthew as a poet expressing theological understanding, rather than as a writer reporting historical facts.

Matthew wants to present Jesus as the fulfillment of Jewish hopes. According to Matthew, Jesus is symbolically reliving the story of Moses, the great leader who was called out of Egypt by God to bring the people toward a new life of freedom. As well, the story of Jesus escaping to Egypt to avoid the murderous intent of King Herod is intended to recall the odyssey of the patriarch Joseph, who was sold into slavery in Egypt by his brothers. (Note the connection between the name of Mary's husband and the tribe of Ephraim, descended from the patriarch Joseph, mentioned earlier on page 14.) Reflect on the extent to which you share the experience of Joseph, scorned and bullied, but yet chosen and favored by God.

An adult reading of the gospel writer's purpose may be seen as complex and too dependent on minor details in the Hebrew Scriptures, but if we settle for a simple understanding of the meaning of the flight into Egypt, we're missing much of the depth and riches of the gospel account. It's worth your effort to explore the profound understandings that are woven into the Bible narratives about the coming of Jesus.

Well-informed adult Christians should understand and respect the *original meaning* of each prophetic allusion in the New Testament (in this case, appreciate the meaning and the beauty of the poetry of Hosea), and then understand and respect how the gospel writer read the passage with new eyes and used it to express the greatness of Jesus, decades after his death and resurrection. Matthew perceived that God was preparing for the Messiah throughout the history of the Jewish people, that Jesus should be understood as the new Moses leading the new people of Israel, and that Jesus somehow also re-lived the experience of the patriarch Joseph who was persecuted by his brothers but later vindicated. Christians of Jewish heritage in Matthew's community were being taught that the life of Jesus "fulfilled" (went beyond) their expectations.

We will return to this episode a little later as we explore Matthew's gospel. The passage from Hosea was dealt with out of order, to set the stage for a discussion of a more well-known prophecy quoted in Matthew 1:23.

3. MATTHEW'S GENEALOGY

Matthew's gospel begins with a genealogy of Jesus, neatly divided into sections from Abraham to King David (roughly 1850—1000 BCE), from David to the deportation to Babylon (970–486 BCE), and from the Babylonian exile to the birth of Jesus. You probably don't need to read every word in the following excerpt, but it is presented for reference, and you will be invited to notice several features in the discussion that follows.

> An account of the genealogy of Jesus the Messiah, the son of David, the son of Abraham. Abraham was the father of Isaac, and Isaac the father of Jacob, and Jacob the father of Judah and his brothers, and Judah the father of Perez and Zerah *by Tamar*, and Perez the father of Hezron, and Hezron the father of Aram, and Aram the father of Aminadab, and Aminadab the father of Nahshon, and Nahshon the father of Salmon, and Salmon the father of Boaz *by Rahab*, and Boaz the father of Obed *by Ruth*, and Obed the father of Jesse, and Jesse the father of King David. And David was the father of Solomon *by the wife of Uriah*, and Solomon the father of Rehoboam, and Rehoboam the father of Abijah . . . and Josiah the father of Jechoniah and his brothers, at the time of the deportation to Babylon. And after the deportation to Babylon: Jechoniah was the father of Salathiel, and Salathiel the father of Zerubbabel . . . and Jacob the father of Joseph the husband of *Mary, of whom Jesus was born*, who is called the Messiah.
>
> So all the generations from Abraham to David are fourteen generations; and from David to the deportation to Babylon, fourteen generations; and from the

deportation to Babylon to the Messiah, fourteen generations. (Excerpts from Matt 1:1–17, emphasis added)

As will be the case with regard to most elements of Matthew's
infancy narrative, the genealogy of Jesus should be understood as
a work of art for a theological purpose, rather than as a historical
document. For example, Matthew 1:17 claims to present fourteen
generations in each of those sections, though they cover unequal
periods of time. A comparison with the genealogy offered in Luke
2:23–38 (which is not part of Luke's infancy narrative, and appears
later in the gospel) shows little similarity except for some famous
biblical figures and two of the kings of Judah. The two lists also
disagree about the name of Jesus's grandfather, Joseph's father.
Whereas Matthew's genealogy traces Jesus's heritage to the original
ancestor of the Jewish people (Abraham), Luke's genealogy, written for a predominantly Gentile Christian community, extends all
the way back to Adam—his way of saying that Jesus is the Savior of
all humanity, not primarily of Jewish people.

Let us now consider the purpose of Matthew's genealogy,
with reference to a number of details in the text.

a) Jesus the Messiah, the Son of David, the Son of Abraham (Matt 1:1)

THE GENEALOGY OF JESUS . . .

The meaning of the name "Jesus" will be dealt with in detail in our
discussion of Matthew 1:21. The name means "God saves" and is
equivalent to the modern English name "Joshua."

. . . THE MESSIAH

Whenever you read the New Testament, be sure to notice the titles
that are given to Jesus. Each of them means something a little

different. Three such titles are listed in the heading of Matthew's genealogy—Messiah, son of David and son of Abraham.

Most people have an understanding of the word *Messiah*—a person who was expected to be sent by God to lead the Jewish people in an ideal age of peace. Because of some familiar prophecies, most Christians associate the Messiah with a king who would set Jewish people free from foreign invaders and establish a utopian kingdom where rivalry and domination would cease, and peace would reign. "The wolf will live with the lamb . . . and the lion shall eat straw like the ox" (Isa 11:6–7).

That hope for political emancipation was predominant among Jews in Jesus's time, but there were other streams of messianic expectation. For example, a hope for a new or renewed covenant was expressed in Jeremiah 31:31–34. There may also have existed a hope for a priest-messiah who would rise from the tribe of Levi. (Remember this when Mary visits her relative, the mother of John the Baptist, in Luke's gospel.) As well, in Matthew's consciousness there likely existed the expectation of a "prophet like Moses." In the book of Deuteronomy, in reporting the death of Moses, the author seems to express a wistful hope with the words, "Never since has there arisen a prophet in Israel like Moses . . ." (Deut 34:10).

The word *meshiach* in Hebrew literally means "anointed" or "the anointed one." Kings and high priests were anointed rather than crowned; a flagon of oil was poured over their head so that it dripped down their beard (Ps 133:2). The Greek word for "anointed" is *christos*, which of course is transliterated into English as Christ. Thus some translations of Matthew 1:1 read "the genealogy of Jesus Christ . . ." That's perfectly accurate, as long as the reader understands that the word Christ means Messiah, a title identifying Jesus as the fulfillment of Jewish hopes. Too many children (and adults!) think that Christ was Jesus's last name![10]

10. Family names were not used in Jesus's society in the same way as they are in our culture, but people were identified by descriptive words beyond their simple given name. Jesus's "family name" (or the descriptor that distinguished him from other Joshuas) probably changed at least three times during his life. When he was growing up, Jesus probably would have been known as his father's son: Yeshua bar Yusif (Joshua son of Joseph, or "Josephson"). After

People also wonder why sometimes the article is inserted into a phrase like "Jesus the Christ." It leads to less misunderstanding if the Greek words *ho christos* in the gospels are translated as "the Messiah" or as "the anointed one."

Matthew 1:1 declares that Jesus was the Messiah that the Jewish people were expecting, and that he fulfilled their hopes, even though he did not achieve political power in his lifetime, and his ministry did not lead to an ideal age of peace in any historical sense.

. . . THE SON OF DAVID

The use of the title "son of David" is a clear statement that Matthew understands Jesus to fulfill the Jewish hope for a great king sent by God. That claim is paradoxical, since Jesus likely did not claim or achieve political power, but Matthew's community believes that Jesus fulfilled the hope for a utopian king in a manner beyond what the Jewish tradition expected. This is another example of reading the Hebrew Scriptures with Christian eyes, and understanding the fulfillment in a different way than the tradition had understood the expectation.

The assertion that Jesus was "son of David" but did not claim to be king is given an ironic twist in the narratives of the last week of Jesus's life. As the episode we remember as Palm Sunday is narrated, when Jesus entered the capital city, Jerusalem, his followers were shouting "Hosanna to the son of David"—a cry certain to be understood as a claim of political kingship. If the gospel reports are accurate, it raises the question why, if Jesus did not aspire to political leadership, he would allow his followers to shout that slogan when it was clearly a challenge to the Caesar. When he

---

Joseph's death, Jesus continued to work at his trade for many years, and he probably would have been known by a "job name"—the carpenter (Mark 6:3). When in time Jesus left his hometown and became a travelling preacher and healer, he was known as "Jesus of Nazareth," the name under which he was crucified. Patronymics and family names derived from employment or place of origin are common in all languages. Consider your own name and those of your friends.

was crucified, the charge over his head, written at Pilate's orders in Latin, Greek and Hebrew, said "Jesus of Nazareth, King of the Jews."[11]

Did Jesus understand that his ministry included a political role, as his followers seem to have expected? If not, why did he allow them to acclaim him as "son of David" during his entry into Jerusalem? We can at least recognize that Jesus knew that the reign of God inevitably has political implications, and that it was a challenge to the tyranny of Rome and Rome's allies in Jesus's homeland. Followers of Jesus today, fighting for human rights and social justice, surely understand their efforts as being faithful to Jesus who dared to attack religious and political power in his society, as a matter of integrity in the proclamation of God's reign.

A related question that must be mentioned under this heading is, "Was Jesus in fact a descendant of David (and perhaps of a series of fourteen Jewish kings), as Matthew's genealogy asserts?" Like so many questions related to Jesus's childhood, this question can only be answered by saying that we have no way of knowing. David (and his successors) had a significant number of wives, concubines and offspring, so it is possible that many people of Jesus's time might have had David as an ancestor, whether they knew it or not.

Certainly, no Christian has claimed that Jesus was the *dauphin*, the heir apparent—the prince who could claim the throne of David by right of inheritance.[12]

Once again, the title "son of David" applied to Jesus in Matthew's genealogy must be understood symbolically rather than historically: according to the Christian community, he fulfills the Jewish hope for a great leader sent by God, but perhaps not

11. In Latin, those words are *Iesus Nazarenus Rex Iudaeorum*, giving us the INRI that used to appear on many artistic depictions of the crucifixion.

12. By the way, neither was King Herod the biological heir to David's throne. Though he practiced Judaism, he was a warlord from an ethnically non-Jewish desert people (the Idumeans or Edomites). Herod took command in the style of modern warlords/dictators, arranged to have Rome proclaim him King of the Jews, and maintained a wealthy and privileged lifestyle as a puppet of Caesar, much hated by his subjects.

necessarily in a biological sense, and only in an adapted political sense: faith in the reign of God has political implications.

. . . THE SON OF ABRAHAM

"Son of Abraham," the third title given to Jesus in the first line of Matthew's genealogy, identifies Jesus as the heir of the promises made to Abraham, who is understood to be the ancestor of all Jewish people. God's promises to Abraham are found in the book of Genesis:

> I will make of you a great nation,
> And I will bless you and make your name great,
> So that you will be a blessing . . .
> In you, all the families of the earth will be blessed. (Gen 12:2–3)

Writing for Christians of predominantly Jewish heritage, Matthew asserts that Jesus is the heir of God's promises to Abraham. The author implicitly reminds his readers that God's benign intentions expressed in the book of Genesis reach far beyond the Jewish community to "all the families of the earth." That theme will recur throughout the gospel, culminating in the assignment given to his followers in the closing verses of the gospel: "Make disciples of all nations" (Matt 28:19).

The Gospel of Matthew begins with a seemingly simple line: "An account of the genealogy of Jesus, the Messiah, the son of David, the son of Abraham" (Matt 1:1). Many paragraphs have been expended to "unpack" the intentions of the gospel writer for just that one line, the title of the genealogy at the beginning of his work. One is moved to wonder, "So what?" What does it matter to twenty-first-century Christians to claim that Jesus was the Jewish Messiah, the son of David, and the heir of the promises to Abraham? The recognition that the reign of God has political implications is an important point for all of us to consider. Otherwise, I don't think those three titles matter very much to most of us. Other assertions later in the infancy narratives can provide significant support to our life of faith. The most one can hope with regard to verse one is that readers are beginning to sense how God was part of the self-understanding of people of Jesus's time, and how God can be part of our lives also.

The other idea that may need mentioning is that the gospel is complex and profound. It is of value for faithful adults to consider the depth of the gospel writer's intentions. Christianity has a tradition of simplifying the gospel, in the middle ages for the benefit of illiterate peasants, in more recent times in order to bring the message of Jesus to children. That is a worthy purpose, but its great disadvantage is that too many adults think that Christians believe (or are supposed to believe) what can be learned before the age of ten. Too many adults have never explored adult theology, and at least partially as a result, regrettably many adults think that believing is only for children. That sentence isn't true of church-goers, but it is true of the very high proportion of adults who rarely or never take part in Christian community life and worship. Christianity is a religion for adults.

b) The Genealogy: Five Women (Matt 1:2–17)

In an unprecedented modification of the traditional art form of genealogy, the author of Matthew has included five women in the list of the ancestors of Jesus. Their names can be found italicized in the passage that is found on page 17. The author's purpose is to point out that God was guiding the history of the people through the centuries, preparing for the coming of Jesus—and that God was able to make use of unusual and sometimes even morally questionable actions of humans to bring about a world-changing outcome.

Contemporary women may find the following stories disconcerting since they took place in a patriarchal culture and often served the purposes of men, but these accounts all tell of women who took strong initiatives to achieve remarkable outcomes—and the gospel writer believes that God was working through the actions of these women (most of them unconventional, some of them not even Jewish) to prepare for God's greatest gift to humanity, the life of Jesus.

The first woman mentioned (in Matt 1:3) is Tamar, who bore the twins Perez and Zerah by the patriarch Judah from whose tribe came David, the greatest king the Jewish people ever had. The chaotic story of Tamar's motherhood is based on an ancient practice known as the Levirate law (see Deut 25:5–10) that was intended to carry on the family name of every married man, even if the man died childless. When a husband died without having sired children, the responsibility of the dead man's brother was to impregnate his sister-in-law, the dead man's widow. The resulting child was understood as the offspring of the dead husband, so that his name would carry on into future generations. According to Genesis 38, Tamar married Er, the son of the patriarch Judah. When her husband died ("put to death by God because of his evil ways," according to the tradition), it was the responsibility of his brother Onan to provide an heir. Presumably out of scorn for his dead brother, Onan refused to sire a child under these circumstances, and earned unending notoriety by "spilling his semen on the ground" rather than impregnating Tamar. After being thus condemned to a life of childless grief, Tamar undertook plan B. Disguised as a prostitute, she seduced her father-in-law Judah, himself now a widower, keeping some identifying chattels from the older man. Later, facing execution for becoming pregnant as a widow, she produced the property of the revered patriarch, identifying him as the father of her twins, and thus preserving the family name of her dead husband. Tamar's initiative earned for her a place in Matthew's unconventional genealogy of Jesus.

The second woman mentioned in Matthew's distinctive family tree of Jesus is Rahab, identified as the mother of Boaz, who was the grandfather of King David (Matt 1:5). Matthew seems to have made a mistake: the mother of Boaz is not identified in the book of Ruth; the only person named Rahab in the Bible was a prostitute (a member of the indigenous residents of the land, not a Jewish woman—see the book of Joshua, chapter 2) who helped the invading Israelites in the time of Joshua, a few centuries before

Boaz lived. All we can say is that Matthew's practice of naming women of unusual reputation as ancestors of Jesus remains intact.

In the same verse (Matt 1:5), Matthew refers to Ruth, a Moabite woman who became the great grandmother of King David. The book of Ruth is short enough that it could be read now in its entirety to see the point of Matthew's reference. Like Tamar's, Ruth's story depends on the Levirate law. In a situation that might be compared to a Jordanian woman marrying a Jewish man in the country of Jordan today, the Moabite woman Ruth found herself a widow in her own homeland, in the company of her widowed Jewish mother-in-law Naomi. Ruth's love and loyalty for Naomi prompts her to return to Naomi's homeland and to adopt Naomi's people and her God, the God of the Jewish people. Naomi arranges for Ruth to seduce and eventually marry a wealthy Jewish kinsman, Boaz, to provide an heir for her late husband. (Understanding of the story is enhanced by the awareness that "feet" was used in Hebrew as a euphemism for male genitals. "She uncovered his feet and lay down" [Ruth 3:7–8].) Thus a resourceful Arab woman became the great grandmother of David, the greatest king of the Jewish people.

The next verse in the gospel refers to "the wife of Uriah." Her name, not given by Matthew, was Bathsheba. She had become David's favorite wife after he had her abducted into his palace, made her pregnant (the child of that rape died shortly after birth), and arranged for the death of her husband Uriah. Bathsheba, benefitting from that sordid series of events, was instrumental in promoting her son Solomon to the throne after the death of his father David (1 Kgs 1:11–31).

The fifth woman named in Matthew's genealogy of Jesus is his mother Mary. Mary actually has a relatively minor role in Matthew's infancy narrative and in the rest of the gospel. She is well-known to us especially because of her role in the Gospel of Luke (which was apparently unknown to Matthew's community when this gospel was written). For Matthew, Mary belongs in the company of the women who have already been mentioned in his genealogy: people who were unexpectedly chosen by God, and who perhaps even have something in their life that causes discomfort. (It seems that the early Christians had to confront a rumor that Jesus was of illegitimate birth; see John 8:41. Both Matthew and Luke portray Mary as being pregnant before marriage, though both assert that the pregnancy was the result of God's action.)

The theological purpose of Matthew's exceptional family tree is to present God as carefully preparing for the coming of the Messiah over many centuries. The Messiah is presented as the descendant of King David and of Abraham, the ancestor of all Jewish people. Further, God is portrayed as making use of human frailty and female ingenuity to bring forth God's greatest gift to humanity, Jesus the Messiah.

4. THE ANNUNCIATION TO JOSEPH

> Now the birth of Jesus the Messiah took place in this way. When his mother Mary had been engaged to Joseph, but before they lived together, she was found to be with child from the Holy Spirit. Her husband Joseph, being a righteous man and unwilling to expose her to public disgrace, planned to dismiss her quietly. But just when he had resolved to do this, an angel of the Lord appeared to him in a dream and said, "Joseph, son of David, do not be afraid to take Mary as your wife, for the child conceived in her is from the Holy Spirit. She will bear a son, and you are to name him Jesus, for he will save his people from their sins." All this took place to fulfill what had been spoken by the Lord through the prophet: "Look, the virgin shall conceive and bear a son, and they shall name him Immanuel," which means, "God is with us." When Joseph awoke from sleep, he did as the angel of the Lord commanded him; he took her as his wife, but had no marital relations with her until she had borne a son; and he named him Jesus. (Matt 1:18–25)

The story of the annunciation to Joseph depends on traditional Jewish marriage practices in which a man and a woman are first betrothed (in those days, usually soon after puberty for the woman; several years later for the male), and later go to live together in the husband's home. Betrothal is a formal step, and sexual unfaithfulness even before the couple began to live together was understood as adultery; the penalty for adultery was death for both partners in the unfaithfulness.

As everyone knows, Mary is portrayed in Matthew's narrative as having become pregnant "by the Holy Spirit," but also apparently as neglecting to tell her husband that she had never been unfaithful. As a "righteous man" who knew only that his betrothed was mysteriously pregnant, by the law of Moses Joseph should have demanded Mary's execution on grounds of adultery, rather than "dismissing her quietly."

Remember, the story that appears in Luke's gospel of an angel announcement to Mary was most likely unknown to Matthew's community; Luke's story may not even have been composed when Matthew's narrative was written. Matthew is making a theological statement about the source and meaning of Jesus's greatness in his own way, using a narrative that may have developed some fifty years after the death and resurrection of Jesus, and more than eighty years after the situation being described. We have no evidence of eyewitness testimony, which could have come only from Joseph, who seems to have died before Jesus's ministry began.[13]

Again, as far as we know, this episode was unknown to any follower of Jesus outside Matthew's community in the first five decades after the resurrection. The purpose of the episode is theological, not historical. It is unfair to demand "historical credibility."

---

13. Jesus is reported to have been about thirty years old when he began his public ministry (Luke 3:23). Statistically, the average life expectancy in Jesus's time was twenty-two years. That average is significantly affected by childhood and maternal mortality, but 90 percent of people died before the age of forty in that era when mortal illness could come at any time without warning or remedy. Joseph could well have married Mary as a young man and have died before the age of forty; Mary must have been in her mid-40s during Jesus's public life. Jesus himself at the age of thirty would be an elder in his community, where he had lived and worked all his life. Some of his contemporaries would be grandparents by that age. The age of thirty in those days might be compared to fifty or sixty now.

An angel of the Lord appeared to him in a dream

In the Scriptures, an angel is a messenger from God. Angels appear in various forms in the ancient texts, often as humans, but at other times they are used as if God is speaking in person directly to the biblical heroes. Genesis 18 begins by saying that God appeared to Abraham, and then says that he saw three men; later in the chapter, Abraham is conversing directly with God. In Genesis 19, two angels come to Sodom, but they soon become men, and later revert to being called angels. Perhaps the best understanding of such accounts is that in conversing with angels, people understand that they are talking and listening to God.

In Matthew's narrative, Joseph is portrayed as sleeping and dreaming, but coming to an understanding of what God is asking of him.

The child is from the Holy Spirit

Matthew's narrative clearly implies that the life of Jesus began by divine creative action. It is not necessary to use a phrase like "without sexual intercourse" to describe it. The gospel writer doesn't use that phrase, but rather repeats that the pregnancy was "from the Holy Spirit." It may be useful to present the "literal meaning" of the episode (but "what is the literal meaning of a poem?"[14]). by reference to the action of God in creating the universe. According to Matthew, the life of Jesus began in Mary's womb by divine creative action.

Joseph comes to understand that he is to continue the marriage process that he and Mary had begun, and to take the formal role of the father in naming the child and thus establishing his place in the genealogy that preceded this episode. The genealogy portrays Jesus as son of David and son of Abraham—of royal heritage and of Jewish ancestry—through Joseph. Still, Matthew is

14. Borg, *Jesus*, 69.

careful in 1:16 to describe Joseph as the husband of Mary rather than as the father of Jesus.

a) You Are to Name Him Jesus for He Will Save His People from Their Sins

YOU ARE TO NAME HIM JESUS

The English name Jesus derives from the Greek version (*Iesous*) of a very common Hebrew name which we know in English as Joshua. In Aramaic, his native language, it may have been pronounced more like Yeshua. The name was quite ordinary; many people in his time as in ours were called Joshua.

Students often ask, "Well, which was it? Was his name Joshua or Jesus?" Certainly, he was not called "Jesus" in his homeland. That word is the English version of the Greek *Iesous*; the gospels were written in Greek. Jesus's hometown didn't speak Greek (or Latin) as its first language. Because of the conquest of Alexander the Great, Greek was still the common language of the Roman Empire in Jesus's time. Jesus spoke Aramaic and understood Hebrew. He may have understood some Greek, as far as it was useful in his work as a tradesman.

The word Joshua in English is closer to Jesus's real name in Hebrew. Realize that many names exist in various forms in different languages.[15] Perhaps it's best to say that the meaning of the

15. In Hebrew, the generic word "God" is *elohim*. The name of God, as revealed to Moses, was Yahweh. Devout Jews have such respect for God's name that they never pronounce it, even when it appears in Bible texts being read in the synagogue. When the name of God appears in the Bible, Jewish readers instead pronounce the word *adonai*, meaning "the Lord." That is why, in most English translations of the Hebrew Bible, the name of God is replaced by LORD, in capital letters. What is actually written in the Hebrew text is the name of God, Yahweh.

Many Hebrew names use the name of God in shortened forms like *Yeho-* or *-iah*. Some examples: The Hebrew name *Yeho-shua* (Joshua) means "Yahweh saves." In other languages the same name appears as Jesus, Iesous, or Gesù.

names Joshua and Jesus are the same; the name takes different forms in different languages.

He will save his people from their sins

The name Joshua, like many Hebrew names, has a religious meaning. *Yeho-shua* means "Yahweh saves." The first two syllables are a form of the never-pronounced name of God, Yahweh; the second half of the name is a form of the verb "to save."

Matthew translates the meaning of Jesus's name for readers of his gospel, so that non-Jewish followers of Jesus could perceive its significance: "for he will save his people from their sins." A valid understanding of that saying should be built on the foundation introduced in the opening chapter of this book: *the good news of the New Testament is that God reaches into our lives and leads us to wholeness.* That action of God is the fundamental meaning of the term "salvation." The meaning of salvation should not be understood primarily in reference to overcoming the "sin of Adam and Eve" or to life after death: "God saves us" means that God leads us to wholeness during our lives, before our death. After Jesus heard the repentant words of the tax collector Zacchaeus in Luke's gospel, he said, "*Today*, salvation has come to this house" (Luke 19:10).

The enterprise in which we are all engaged is actually building our *selves* by our decisions, day after day, in big decisions or by habitual and perhaps almost unrecognized good deeds. ("Virtue" is defined as the habit of doing good.) The gospel teaches that wholeness (personal fulfillment) is possible because the saving action of God overcomes our sinfulness, heals us and renews us on the path toward wholeness.

Notice that there is no sign in the gospel (or in the previous explanation) of the God who was so enraged at the sin of Adam and Eve that he held a grudge against all humanity and demanded

---

Yeho-hanan means "Yahweh is gracious." Translations into other languages include John, Johann, Juan, Sean, Ian, Ivan, Giovanni, and for women, Jean, Joanne, Juanita, Giovanna, Seanna, Yvonne, and Ivana. *Yeho-nathan* (Jonathan) means "gift of Yahweh."

the death of his beloved Son to repay the debt of the "original sin." That doctrine, so detrimental to a valid understanding of the saving action of God, is unknown in Jewish tradition and in the gospels; it is the creation of later Christian theology.[16] In the Bible, God is entirely on our side, taking action to help us. Even demanding moral teaching in the Scriptures is understood as *wisdom* to enlighten us about what is truly best for us.

"Sin" includes whatever we do that leads us away from wholeness; sin refers to decisions we make that are untrue to who we really are and therefore unfaithful to God's call to wholeness.

In the setting of Matthew's infancy narrative, Jesus is presented as the gift of God who will overcome our sinfulness and lead us to wholeness, if we are willing to accept God's saving influence. That is the pivotal theological insight to be sought in this episode. The story is not primarily about Mary; it is about what God can do for us through the life of Jesus. It is the ultimate "so what?" statement of Matthew's infancy narrative: "He will save his people from their sins."

b) The Virgin Shall Conceive

At this point, Matthew inserts in the story one of his typical fulfillment sayings, quoting the prophet Isaiah 7:14. Our earlier discussion of Hosea 11:1 (quoted in Matt 2:15) was intended to provide the background necessary for an understanding of this famous

---

16. Contemporary theology of salvation or "soteriology" has a profound and beautiful understanding of the saving action of God that is not based on the "original sin." In addition to the paragraphs above, I have tried to summarize it in the final chapter of my book *Language of the Heart*, entitled "Jesus Lived, Died, and Rose to Save Us from Our Sins." My first extensive learning about soteriology was in a course given more than forty years ago by Stanislas Lyonnet, SJ, whose name and work can be found with an internet search. The medieval idea of a vengeful God demanding the death of his beloved Son is far from the biblical (Old and New Testament) idea of a saving God of steadfast love, who forgives and overcomes our sinfulness and leads us towards wholeness.

passage. We will begin with a discussion of the quoted text in its original context.

> Again the Lord spoke to Ahaz, saying, "Ask a sign of the Lord your God; let it be deep as Sheol or high as heaven." But Ahaz said, "I will not ask, and I will not put the Lord to the test." Then Isaiah said: "Hear then, O house of David! Is it too little for you to weary mortals, that you weary my God also? Therefore the Lord himself will give you a sign. Look, the young woman is with child and shall bear a son, and shall name him Immanuel." (Isa 7:10–14)

As we did for Hosea, we must explore the original meaning of the passage, then its interpretation in later Jewish history, and finally its re-understanding when Christians, after Jesus's resurrection, re-interpreted it with the eyes of "fulfillment."

The original context of the saying is a dispute between the prophet and Ahaz, the king of Judah (the small southern kingdom). Isaiah had been trying to persuade King Ahaz to be a leader who was faithful to the demands of God, but Ahaz would have nothing to do with this religious activist. Isaiah offers Ahaz a sign of the king's choosing just to prove that God is real and powerful, but the king refuses, with an excuse that he doesn't want to test God. Isaiah then says, "God is going to give you a sign whether you want it or not," and pronounces the famous oracle, "A young woman is with child, and will bear a son, and shall name him Immanuel."

The Hebrew word used by Isaiah is *almah*, meaning "a young woman of marriageable age." Other possible English translations include "maiden" or "damsel." The specific Hebrew word for "virgin" is *bethulah*. The scholarly Protestant-Catholic committee that produced the New Revised Standard Version, which is widely recognized as the best academic translation of the Bible, chose the term "young woman" to render the meaning of *almah* in Isaiah 7:14.

Most Christian scholars agree that Isaiah's oracle is a forceful reminder to the king that he is mortal. Quite possibly the "young woman" is the queen, the king's young wife. Isaiah warns Ahaz that he is going to die, that the child to be born will succeed him, and that the next king will be faithful to God, unlike his father. In history, the king after Ahaz was Hezekiah (715–687 BCE), who was indeed a religious reformer. But after those reforms, and relapses and reforms by subsequent Jewish kings, the people began to realize that none of these crowned heads was worthy of being called "God with us," the literal meaning of the name Immanuel.[17] Thus there developed in Jewish tradition an expectation of a future great king who would indeed be truly faithful to God and would inaugurate a lasting reign of peace and prosperity—the messianic kingdom. It is that hope that Matthew proclaims as having been fulfilled in the life of Jesus.

One further unexpected development in the understanding of this passage took place in the pre-Christian history of Isaiah 7:14. Some three centuries before Jesus lived, many Jewish people had emigrated from Palestine and settled all around the Mediterranean Sea. The language of the Mediterranean world, thanks to Alexander the Great, was Greek; many Jews had lived away from their homeland for generations, and could not understand their Scriptures in Hebrew. Scholars in Alexandria, Egypt (note the derivation of the city's name) undertook to translate the Hebrew Scriptures into the language of the empire. We have their translation, known as the Septuagint, in its entirety; scholars compare it with what we know of the original Hebrew text (which itself was evolving through the centuries). For no reason that we know of, in Isaiah 7:14 the Alexandrian scholars translated the Hebrew word *almah*, meaning "young woman," by the Greek word *parthenos*, meaning "virgin." Most Christian scholars agree that "virgin" is not what is meant by the Hebrew word in Isaiah 7:14. However, Matthew was writing his gospel in Greek and was reading the book of Isaiah in Septuagint Greek, so he saw, "A virgin shall conceive."

---

17. In Hebrew, *imma* means "with"; *nu* means "us"; *el* is the shortened form of the word *elohim*, meaning "God." Notice that the next king wasn't literally named Immanuel. Neither was Jesus, though Matthew presents him as fulfilling God's promise to be with us.

Understanding the passage with Christian eyes, he proclaimed that Jesus was born of a virgin, in fulfillment of the passage in the prophet Isaiah.

Part of the goal in saying that Jesus was born of a virgin is to surpass the miraculous conception of numerous other heroes of Jewish history. "Childhood stories of the heroes" is a familiar art form that often included conception after decades of barrenness or when the parents were so old that only the action of God could give them a child. No other Jewish hero, however, is virginally conceived. As well, Matthew is probably presenting Jesus in competition with Greek and Roman mythology (with its frequent god-human offspring) and with the Caesars who claimed titles like Son of God and Savior for themselves.

Both gospel narratives about Jesus's childhood assert that the creative action of God was even greater in the conception of Jesus than it ever had been in Jewish tradition. These narratives emphasize the action of God in giving us the life of Jesus: humanity must not claim credit for the greatness of Jesus; he is not simply the greatest product of his Jewish heritage. From a Christian point of view, the life of Jesus is the direct gift of God.

Whether one accepts Matthew's proclamation of virgin conception[18] as historically accurate or not, the passage is intended to be a declaration about the positive intervention of God and about the greatness of Jesus. It is Jesus, not the kings who suc-

18. Note that contemporary media and many believers use the term "Immaculate Conception" in error to refer to the virginal conception of Jesus. The distinctive (and nonbiblical) Catholic doctrine of Immaculate Conception is about the conception of *Mary* in her mother's womb—not a virginal conception, but a conception without the "stain" of original sin, as that doctrine was understood when the Immaculate Conception teaching was developed a few centuries ago. For reassurance about this statement about the meaning of Immaculate Conception (which many faithful but uninformed Catholics consider to be mistaken), notice that the celebration of Mary's Immaculate Conception takes place on December 8 every year; her "birthday" is celebrated on September 8, nine months later. Jesus's "birthday" is of course celebrated on December 25; his *conception* is celebrated on March 25, nine months earlier. That commemoration is known as the Annunciation (not "Immaculate Conception"), recalling the angel's announcement to Mary of the forthcoming birth of her child, as reported in the Gospel of Luke.

ceeded Ahaz, who is truly "God with us" (the literal translation of Immanuel, provided by Matthew for his Greek readers who don't understand Hebrew). It is Jesus who is God's gift to humanity, carrying on God's action of salvation, overcoming human sinfulness and leading us to wholeness.

The "Immanuel" reference in Matthew's overture is brought to completion at the end of the gospel, when Jesus, having conquered death, gives a worldwide commission to his followers ("Make disciples of all nations.") and *doesn't* bid them farewell, but promises to be *with* them always, "to the end of the age" (Matt 28:20). The author reminds Christians through the ages that Jesus still remains Immanuel, "God with us."

HE TOOK HER AS HIS WIFE

The episode ends when Joseph awakens from his dream, and does what God has asked him to do: he takes Mary into his home (step two of the marriage process), has no marital relations with her until the child is born, and undertakes the formal naming which establishes Jesus as son of David and son of Abraham.

5. THE MAGI COME TO JERUSALEM

Chapter 2 of Matthew's gospel presents five scenes that are so familiar to believers that they are usually taken as one (and often harmonized with Luke's infancy narrative to such an extent that children will mistakenly say that the shepherds followed the star to find where the baby was born).

Matthew's five scenes are the following: the magi come to Jerusalem and are directed to Bethlehem; the magi follow the star to the house, pay homage and go home by another route; the family flees to Egypt; the male children of Bethlehem are killed at Herod's command; and the family migrates to Nazareth.

We will discuss each of those episodes in some detail.

> In the time of King Herod, after Jesus was born in Bethlehem of Judea, wise men from the East came to Jerusalem, asking, "Where is the child who has been born king of the Jews? For we observed his star at its rising, and have come to pay him homage." When King Herod heard this, he was frightened, and all Jerusalem with him; and calling together all the chief priests and scribes of the people, he inquired of them where the Messiah was to be born. They told him, "In Bethlehem of Judea; for so it has been written by the prophet: 'And you, Bethlehem, in the land of Judah, are by no means least among the rulers of Judah; for from you shall come a ruler who is to shepherd my people Israel.'" Then Herod secretly called for the wise men and learned from them the exact time when the star had appeared. Then he sent them to Bethlehem, saying, "Go and search diligently for the child; and when you have found him, bring me word so that I may also go and pay him homage." (Matt 2:1–8)

In the time of King Herod . . .

Two kings named Herod have important roles in the gospels. King Herod "the Great" was alive when Jesus was born according to both Matthew and Luke. Historians agree that Herod died in 4 BCE, so Jesus was likely born before that year.[19] Herod the Great was hated by his subjects. He was not ethnically Jewish, but a self-declared potentate from Idumea (or Edom) who was able to live as the king of the Jews because he served the Romans as their puppet. Like Solomon a thousand years earlier, he imposed conscription and forced the young conscripts into slave labor, making them build palaces and forts for him away from Jerusalem. One of them was

19. Our system of dating the years "from the birth of Jesus" was developed several centuries after Jesus lived, by a monk who tried to estimate when Jesus was born by calculating back through the reigns of various emperors and kings. (For example, Luke 3:1 says that the ministry of John the Baptist began in the fifteenth year of the reign of the emperor Tiberias.) The monk whose research concluded that Jesus was born in what we now call "the year 1" miscalculated by a matter of four to six years.

the cliff-top fort near the Dead Sea called Masada, where Herod liked to go for vacations. In the course of a rebellion against the Roman Empire around the year 70 CE, more than seventy years after the death of Herod the Great, several heroic Jewish warriors took shelter at Masada and held off the Roman army for some years. Eventually they all committed suicide just before they were overrun. Another desert palace, Herodium, was built for Herod in sight of Bethlehem and not far from Jerusalem; it is thought that Herod's remains are buried somewhere in the foundations of that cone-shaped fortification.

After King Herod the Great died, his kingdom was divided among his four sons, who were called tetrarchs—rulers of one-quarter of the kingdom. (*Tetra* is the Greek word for four.) The tetrarch of Galilee when Jesus lived there was Herod Antipas, one of Herod's sons. Matthew 14:6–11 reports that Herod Antipas ordered the death of John the Baptist, who had spoken against Antipas's divorce of his wife and marriage to his brother Philip's divorced wife, Herodias. According to Luke 23:5–12, the tetrarch Herod Antipas, ruler of Galilee, happened to be in Jerusalem when Jesus was arrested, and Pontius Pilate tried to get Herod Antipas to take responsibility for Jesus because Jesus was Galilean. Jesus refused to talk to Herod (you may remember the scene as it was portrayed in *Jesus Christ Superstar*), so Herod sent him back to Pilate.

... AFTER JESUS WAS BORN IN BETHLEHEM OF JUDEA ...

Matthew relegates the birth of Jesus to a subordinate clause in his account, and goes on to relate the episode of the coming of the magi. One interesting detail in Matthew's narrative indicates that the author had not heard of Luke's narrative about census or stable. Putting together Matthew 1:24 (literally, "he took Mary into his house"), 2:1 ("born in Bethlehem of Judea") and 2:11 ("entering the house they saw the child"), it seems that Matthew's testimony is that Joseph and Mary lived in Bethlehem, and that Jesus was born in Joseph's house in that town.

Today, on the other side of Bethlehem from the Church of the Nativity (which is based on Luke's gospel), Syrian Catholics preserve the memory of Joseph's home where Matthew's gospel reports that Jesus was born. According to Matthew, when the family migrates to Nazareth after their Egyptian adventure, they have moved away from their home and Jesus's birthplace for fear of the authorities in Jerusalem.

... Magi from the East came to Jerusalem ...

A *magos* is a seer or wizard; the word magician is derived from the same root. Most scholars think that Matthew had astrologers in mind because the East, probably meaning Persia, had an air of mystery. The gospel writer probably wasn't thinking about kings, although thoughtful readers have perceived echoes of Psalm 72:10—"May the kings of Tarshish and of the isles render him tribute, / May the kings of Sheba and Seba bring gifts." Nothing except the number of gifts indicates how many magi came to visit the child. Since women could be astrologers, the phrase "wise men" is unnecessarily gender exclusive; "sages" would be a more inclusive translation of the original Greek word *magoi*.

The central matter of interest about the magi is their open-minded willingness to learn and to change. Writing for a Christian community predominantly of Jewish heritage, Matthew tells about open-minded people who are *not* Jewish, but who search for truth and are open to portents that would indicate the arrival of a great leader.

In this first scene of the narrative, they arrive in Jerusalem as a result of noticing "his star at its rising" and inquire from authorities there about the "newborn king." Herod is presented as being unaware of messianic expectations; his Jerusalem advisors consult their scriptural sources about the hoped-for Messiah, and advise the magi where to search further.

. . . YOU, BETHLEHEM IN THE LAND OF JUDAH . . .

> And you, Bethlehem, in the land of Judah, are by no
> means least among the rulers of Judah; for from you shall
> come a ruler who is to shepherd my people Israel.

Matthew quotes from the prophet Micah 5:2 (with a phrase added from 2 Sam 5:2) to support the belief that the Messiah was to come from Bethlehem. The original meaning of the Micah verse refers to the long-held hope for an ideal king in the spirit of David; it may not have been intended as a literal prediction that the Messiah would be born in Bethlehem, though that verse likely did give rise to the early Christian tradition that Jesus was born in Bethlehem. To attain a more poetic, less literal sense about the meaning of such verses, recall our earlier discussion of Isaiah 7:14: "They shall name him Immanuel." Neither King Ahaz's son Hezekiah (in the original meaning of the oracle) nor the Messiah was literally given the name "Immanuel," but both were in different ways, poetically, "God with us." Similarly, Micah's saying about a future great ruler coming out of Bethlehem may have expressed the hope for a king in the spirit of David.

The idea that Jesus was born in Bethlehem was apparently unknown to Paul or Mark; they presume that Jesus came from Nazareth. It is possible that the claim is the result of re-reading with Christian eyes certain prophetic passages (like Mic 5:2) connecting the Messiah to the birthplace of King David. Even Catholic scholars now debate the historical reliability of the two gospels' assertion that Jesus was born in Bethlehem, and some end with the usual disclaimer, "We have no way of knowing for sure."

6. THE VISIT OF THE MAGI

> When they had heard the king, they set out; and there,
> ahead of them, went the star that they had seen at its
> rising, until it stopped over the place where the child
> was. When they saw that the star had stopped, they were
> overwhelmed with joy. On entering the house, they saw

the child with Mary his mother; and they knelt down and paid him homage. Then, opening their treasure chests, they offered him gifts of gold, frankincense, and myrrh. And having been warned in a dream not to return to Herod, they left for their own country by another road. (Matt 2:9–12)

THE STAR . . . STOPPED OVER THE PLACE WHERE THE CHILD WAS

Apparently the original star directed the sages only to the capital city of Jerusalem, but after they received additional information from the Jewish authorities, the star led them onward to Bethlehem and directly to the house where the child could be found.

Please try to erase questions from your mind that depend on reading this narrative literally. Rather, appreciate it as a symbolic story. Suspend your literalistic skepticism. If a child asks questions like, "Why couldn't the star lead them directly to the child in the first place? How does a star lead you to a city or a specific house? Does the story imply that they travelled only at night?," try to help the child understand that the story is not intended to be factual; it is intended to express truth about God and Jesus in the form of a story.

The magi pay homage to the child, and present their treasures. Their gifts, in keeping with Christian understanding of the greatness of Jesus, are symbolic: gold (for a king), frankincense (the fragrant smoke rising to heaven like prayer) and myrrh (used in the burial process, focusing on the future death of the child).

The author of the gospel undoubtedly intended readers to hear echoes of an uplifting passage in Isaiah, originally written to encourage Jews who had returned from exile in Babylon, and were trying to re-establish their civilization in the ruins of their homeland. This passage also mentions kings, but the gospel calls the visitors only *magoi*.

Arise, shine, for your light has come,
and the glory of the LORD has risen upon you. . .

Nations shall come to your light,
and kings to the brightness of your dawn. . .
The wealth of the nations shall come to you.
A multitude of camels shall cover you. . .
They shall bring gold and frankincense
and shall proclaim the praise of the LORD. (Isa 60:1–6)

Then after being warned in a dream, the magi head for home by another road, and are never mentioned again in the New Testament. It is a charming story.

The "so what?" of this segment of the narrative could be based on the association of us Christians to the characteristics of the magi. Like the magi, we hope to be open to truth wherever it is found; we seek to open our hearts to the reign of God, and ask ourselves where God is trying to take us in certain situations. At times we may need to be willing to leave the familiar behind and search for potential value in unexpected places. Perhaps today's magi are immigrants, who have left their homes, friendships, and even families, and sought fulfillment in a new homeland; perhaps they are searchers who have left traditional beliefs or relationships behind and sought to understand life in a new way. In what ways have you been a searcher in your life?

One of the great poets of the twentieth century, T. S. Eliot, wrote a poem about the hardships of the search for truth. "Journey of the Magi" was written after the poet had left the religious community of his childhood and accepted Anglicanism. In the poem, one of the magi speaks in the first person, expressing wistful nostalgia for places left behind as he faces the hardships of the journey, and the distractions and discomforts that are part of the process. As the magi arrive in a temperate valley that was the goal of their odyssey, the poet speaks of the disenchantment of finding your dream: the "three trees" recall the three crosses that marked the end of Jesus's earthly journey and the corruption that destroys the dream and makes the achievement no better than "satisfactory"— a word which may also imply atonement. In the end, the magus returns to his former haunts, but realizes that "you can't go home again," because the meaning of home has changed irrevocably as a result of the journey, and "another death" may be the best hope.

Many of us have lived aspects of the journey of the magi as Eliot imagined it. The text of the poem "The Journey of the Magi" can be found using a simple internet search.[20]

7. THE ESCAPE TO EGYPT

> Now after they had left, an angel of the Lord appeared to Joseph in a dream and said, "Get up, take the child and his mother, and flee to Egypt, and remain there until I tell you; for Herod is about to search for the child, to destroy him." Then Joseph got up, took the child and his mother by night, and went to Egypt, and remained there until the death of Herod. This was to fulfill what had been spoken by the Lord through the prophet, "Out of Egypt I have called my son." (Matt 2:13–15)

As mentioned under heading 2 in this chapter, this brief paragraph (including the fulfillment citation) is used by Matthew to establish that Jesus is reliving the history of his people, first in following the patriarch Joseph to Egypt as a result of the evil intentions of his brothers, and then in imitating Moses who brought his people out of Egypt and who, after an encounter with God on Mount Sinai, established the religious way of life that is enshrined in the law of Moses. The Gospel of Matthew presents Jesus as personifying the new Moses, and proclaiming a new "law" from a new mountain.[21]

Although such echoes of the Hebrew Scriptures are of little relevance to most Christians today, we may still be able to find a place for ourselves in the narrative, if in any way we can consider ourselves refugees, as the family of Jesus surely was, leaving their

20. You can listen to T. S. Eliot reading his own poem at http://www. poetryarchive.org/poetryarchive/singlePoem.do?poemId=7070. Read it reflectively.

21. The Sermon on the Mount is found only in Matthew chapters 5–7, though Luke 6:17–49 has a similar collection of sayings in a speech that takes place on "level ground."

home to evade a threat to their lives. Many people in today's world did indeed flee their homes to avoid oppression, but many others might consider themselves similar to refugees without ever leaving home: people who have been victims of domestic violence, sexual abuse, serious depression, bullying or discrimination on the basis of race or sexual orientation or any other pretext, have shared the helpless experience of Joseph and Mary. There will be no angelic intervention to overcome such threats, but there may be some measure of relief in the faith that the spiritual saving action of God proclaimed in the gospel is directed to helping us deal with such perils with wisdom, courage and love. No matter what happens to us, says the gospel, God supports our inner lives and enables us to grow to wholeness in spite of adverse circumstances.

8. THE MASSACRE OF THE CHILDREN

> When Herod saw that he had been tricked by the wise men, he was infuriated, and he sent and killed all the children in and around Bethlehem who were two years old or under, according to the time that he had learned from the wise men. Then was fulfilled what had been spoken through the prophet Jeremiah: "A voice was heard in Ramah, wailing and loud lamentation, Rachel weeping for her children; she refused to be consoled, because they are no more." (Matt 2:16–18)

The childhood stories of heroes, in the Bible and in other cultures, usually include an episode where the life of the hero is threatened but then preserved by miraculous intervention. Recall in particular the threat to the child Moses by the Pharaoh who demanded the death of all male Hebrew children; Moses's life was saved by the clever action of his mother and sister, who hid him in bulrushes until he was discovered and adopted by an Egyptian princess.

In Matthew's gospel, the Pharaoh's role is played by King Herod; Jesus, of course, is the new Moses. As well, readers are expected to notice the contrast between the open-minded sages from far away who search out and pay homage to Jesus, and the Jewish ruler who rejects Jesus and takes monstrous measures to eliminate this threat to his power.

We have reasonably extensive historical records about the reign of Herod the Great, but there is no record of this particular attack on the male infants of Bethlehem. Such an action would not be impossible for Herod, who for example ensured that the whole nation would be weeping at his death by instructing his guards to gather the nobles of the nation into a stadium, announce his passing, and then execute all of them.

Whether the massacre of the boys of Bethlehem is historical or not, the lesson for us readers is clear. We prefer to consider ourselves as modern-day magi, searching for truth and accepting Jesus and his gospel. The challenge to our self-satisfaction in this episode is the possibility that in our way of life we are more like the Pharaoh or Herod, giving lip-service to the gospel, but in fact being dedicated to preserving our own power and comfort even at mortal cost to others.

Jesus spoke about the dangers of money remarkably often. (He almost never talked about sex, by the way.) He knew that economic concerns are of major importance to most people, and especially to those who are in need. His teaching was remarkably radical in attacking the rich and powerful, and supporting the poor.

We in North America are far more powerful and wealthy than the vast majority of people in the world, yet we continue to wage war in pursuit of fossil fuel, to damage the environment because we refuse to accept the limitations on our lifestyle that would be involved in reducing carbon emissions, and to buy goods that were manufactured by workers, some of them children, whose pay for a day approximates what we are paid for a few minutes' work. Even the poor in first-world countries are more prosperous than millions of people who live in "emerging economies." As a person who lives successfully in the North American middle class, I honestly don't know how to be a faithful Christian in this society. I'm sure that my annual donations to food banks and other charities do not permit me to think that I am living in keeping with the gospel's insistence on the dangers of wealth.

If the Pharaoh and Herod are symbols of ruthless power, each of us followers of Jesus has to face the challenge: do we accept Jesus's gospel standards, or are we more like Herod, dedicated to preserving our own comfort? What would we do if we truly opened our heart to the reign of God? The season of Advent exists so that we can ask such questions of ourselves.

. . . RACHEL WEEPING FOR HER CHILDREN

In the episode of the murder of the boy babies in Bethlehem, Matthew hears an echo of a verse from the book of the prophet Jeremiah (31:15). It could be worthwhile to read the entire chapter, Jeremiah 31, and to experience the meaning of that verse in its original context. Jeremiah both foresaw and lived through the destruction of Jerusalem in 586 BCE and the subsequent exile of many citizens in Babylon, and his writing expressed his deep distress at the events that befell his people. Chapter 31, however, is one of the most beautiful and uplifting passages in the book. In verse 3, God says to the people, "I have loved you with an everlasting love; therefore I have continued my faithfulness to you."

The verse that is quoted in the Gospel of Matthew is an expression of profound grief about the death of so many Jewish people in those traumatic events, but it leads very quickly to a beautiful and consoling message:

> Thus says the LORD:
> Keep your voice from weeping and your eyes from tears
> . . .
> There is hope for your future, says the LORD:
> Your children shall come back to their own country."

Toward the end of Jeremiah chapter 31 is found one of the most significant and hopeful prophecies in the Jewish Scriptures:

> The days are surely coming, says the Lord, when I will make a new covenant with the house of Israel and the

> house of Judah ... But this is the covenant that I will
> make with the house of Israel after those days, says the
> LORD: I will put my law within them, and I will write
> it on their hearts; and I will be their God, and they shall
> be my people. No longer shall they teach one another,
> or say to each other, "Know the Lord," for they shall all
> know me, from the least of them to the greatest, says the
> Lord; for I will forgive their iniquity, and remember their
> sin no more.

Living in a situation of intense suffering, the prophet speaks of hope, of a covenant based on God's forgiveness to be written in human hearts, resulting in a true experience of God within us.

Reflecting on an account of mindless murder in the story of the childhood of Jesus, Matthew recalls the lowest point in Jewish history, and invites readers to accept the reign of God within their hearts. People who have experienced profound distress may recognize that the gospel does not promise that God will take away the suffering, but rather that in opening our hearts to the action of God, we may grow in peace, wisdom, courage and hope.

9. MIGRATION TO NAZARETH

> When Herod died, an angel of the Lord suddenly ap-
> peared in a dream to Joseph in Egypt and said, "Get up,
> take the child and his mother, and go to the land of Israel,
> for those who were seeking the child's life are dead." Then
> Joseph got up, took the child and his mother, and went
> to the land of Israel. But when he heard that Archelaus
> was ruling over Judea in place of his father Herod, he was
> afraid to go there. And after being warned in a dream, he
> went away to the district of Galilee. There he made his
> home in a town called Nazareth, so that what had been
> spoken through the prophets might be fulfilled, "He will
> be called a Nazorean." (Matt 2:19–23)

Matthew's infancy narrative comes to an end after the death of King Herod, with Joseph being guided by two more dream-events to return to his native land but not to his home in Bethlehem. The story has thus dealt with the late first-century Christian understanding that Jesus was born in Bethlehem in the south, but that he grew up in the northern province of Galilee, and was henceforth known as Jesus of Nazareth.

The fulfillment saying which concludes Matthew's infancy narrative is unfathomable: no such saying can be found in the Hebrew Scriptures, and scholars have expended much effort seeking the meaning and derivation of "Nazorean." The inquiry has no relevance to the life of the contemporary Christian believer.

10. CONCLUSION

And thus the stage is set. In chapter 3 of Matthew, John the Baptist begins preaching in the wilderness of Judea, and Jesus comes from his home in Galilee to accept baptism as a sign of his conversion from ordinary small-town tradesman to proclaimer of the reign of God. His public ministry is about to begin.

The author of the gospel according to Matthew has initiated a number of themes that will be carried forward into the body of the gospel. Jesus has been presented as God's gift to humanity, God with us, who will be accepted or rejected on the basis of people's personal attitudes to life and faith. Everyone has been invited to open their heart to the good news and to God's offer to transform our lives and to lead us toward wholeness. Those themes will be central to the entire gospel.

Chapter 3

The Christmas Stories in Luke

1. INTRODUCTION

As we begin the discussion of the Christmas stories in Luke, it might be useful to review the introductory chapter in this book, which is summarized briefly in the following paragraphs.

The first point to remember is that Jesus's most important teaching was, "The reign of God has come . . . The reign of God is upon you . . . The reign of God is within you." That phrase is a proclamation that if we will allow God to reign in our hearts, God will transform us and give us the spiritual energy to live in love, to meet life's challenges with wisdom and courage, and ultimately to be true to ourselves and to God as we create our selves by our decisions. All those phrases are synonymous with the statement "God saves us." "God saves us," means that God reaches into our lives, overcomes our failings, and leads us to wholeness. That transformation will happen to the extent that we open our hearts to the reign of God.

The second introductory segment is a brief history of the development of the New Testament. The authentic letters of Paul were complete and Paul had died before any gospel was written. The earliest gospel was Mark, written in the early 70s of the first Christian century. Neither of those authors is aware of any information that appears in what we know as the infancy narratives. Later, the Gospel of Matthew was written in the early 80s; its author likely was not aware of what we read about Jesus's birth in the Gospel of Luke; Luke's gospel had not yet been written. Matthew's narrative includes a genealogy of Jesus and accounts of an angel's message to Joseph, the visit of the magi, the flight to Egypt, the massacre of the boy children in Bethlehem and the migration of the family of Jesus to Nazareth. Each segment of the narrative has a distinctive purpose as an introduction to themes that are expanded in the rest of the gospel, and that have relevance for Christian believers today. The Gospel of Luke was written near the year 90 CE. As far as scholars can tell, the author of Luke had not read Matthew, and so was not familiar with Matthew's genealogy, or the episodes that are narrated in Matthew's gospel.

Any items in the infancy narratives on which the two gospels agree may be understood as the product of tradition that dates back to a time before either gospel was completed. Such points of agreement include that Jesus was born during the reigns of Herod the Great and Augustus Caesar, that he was understood to be a descendant of David, that he was born in David's birthplace, that his mother's name was Mary and that her husband's name was Joseph, that Mary conceived her child before she was fully married to Joseph, and that Jesus was conceived as the result of a creative act of God.

With that background renewed, we advance to a discussion of the infancy narrative in the gospel according to Luke.

2. CHARACTERISTICS OF LUKE'S COMMUNITY AND THE GOSPEL

The Gospel of Luke was probably written in the late 80s or early 90s of the first century. The Gospel of Matthew had been written by then, but many scholars believe that it was not known in the community where Luke's gospel was composed. The author of Luke made use of a number of sources, including the Gospel of Mark, the sayings collection that we know as Q, other written materials, and of course the oral form of the tradition as it was preserved in that locality—as well as the author's own understanding of the value of Jesus's good news.

The original audience for the Gospel of Luke was a community of Christians who were "people of the Roman Empire"—they had little interest in the Jewish heritage of Jesus, but were followers of his message of faith and his challenging moral standards. Those of us who are of Gentile rather than of Jewish heritage could consider that the Gospel of Luke is addressed to us in a special way.

It is widely agreed that we don't know the name of the author of the gospel. The document's traditional attribution to Luke the physician, who is named in Colossians 4:4 and 2 Timothy 4:11 (two documents that were likely composed after the death of Paul by unknown writers), is not part of the original scroll. The attribution is first documented in *Adversus Haereses* by Iranaeus, ca. 180 CE.

It is also agreed that the same author wrote both the gospel according to Luke and the Acts of the Apostles, the fifth book of the New Testament, a narrative of the first three decades of Christianity and in particular of the missionary activity of Paul (composed some five decades after the events it describes).

The author of Luke was capable of writing elegant Greek, as seen in the first four verses of the gospel. His dedication to his patron Theophilus is a single grammatically correct complex sentence. The narratives that follow it use a much simpler style, similar in some ways to Jewish storytelling—an observation which causes some commentators to suggest that the infancy narratives may have been written by someone else and adopted as a source by Luke, while others see the variety of writing styles in the gospel as an example of Luke's creative skill.

Three characteristics of the Gospel of Luke deserve to be mentioned in this introduction. Each of them is introduced in the infancy narratives, and continues throughout the gospel.

- Jesus is presented as very radical in his attacks on the rich and his support for the poor. One of many examples reads, "None of you can become my disciple if you do not give up all your possessions" (Luke 14:33).

- The Holy Spirit is deeply involved as a powerful influence on the life of Jesus; Jesus often prays for divine support in facing significant decisions in his life.

- Women (including Mary and later Mary Magdalene) play a significant role in the life of Jesus and are treated with respect and friendship in this gospel more than in others.

3. STRUCTURE OF THE INFANCY NARRATIVE IN LUKE

Luke's narrative of the conception, birth and childhood of Jesus is considerably more complex than Matthew's infancy narrative; Luke's version includes accounts of the conception and birth of John the Baptist. Scholars debate about the author's intended organization, but the following structure seems to express the parallels adequately:

- *Section 1*: annunciation to Zachary about the conception of John the Baptist; annunciation to Mary about the conception of Jesus; the two strands brought together in the episode of Mary's visit to Elizabeth.

- *Section 2*: the birth and naming of JBap;[22] the birth and naming of Jesus; the follow-up account of the parents' trip to the temple (for rites of redemption of the first-born and purification of the mother).

- *Concluding episode*: the scene about Jesus as a young man in the temple.

As was said about Matthew's infancy narrative, the accounts in Luke should be understood for their theological purpose more

22. The abbreviation JBap will be used for John the Baptist, since he will be referred to frequently. The abbreviation also serves to distinguish JBap from Jesus's disciple, John the son of Zebedee, and from the purported authors of the Gospel of John, the letters of John, and the book of Revelation.

than their historical reliability. These stories probably took their final form almost ninety years after the events they describe. The author likely had no knowledge of Matthew's narrative, but relied on traditions (some perhaps written by unknown authors before the gospel itself) that had arisen within his community. The two gospels' versions of the Christmas stories are practically incompatible, as Luke portrays the home of Mary to be in Nazareth, while Matthew portrays the couple as residents of Bethlehem; Luke centers several episodes around the capital city Jerusalem, while Matthew says that "all Jerusalem" was frightened at the news of the birth, and that the authorities in Jerusalem were trying to murder the child. Even some Roman Catholic scholars realize that it is unlikely that Mary is the source of Luke's tradition. In particular, the census referred to in Luke happened at least ten years after the birth of Jesus, so Mary could not have told of it as the reason for their journey to Bethlehem. In my opinion, the two gospel overtures should be understood as two separate compositions expressing the authors' understanding of the greatness of Jesus by focusing on his birth and early life—a time about which we have no eyewitness evidence.

Luke's version of the genealogy of Jesus is not part of his infancy narrative, since it appears in the body of the gospel, after the account of Jesus's baptism by JBap. As a result, we won't deal with Luke's genealogy in this chapter, but we can state that it differs almost completely from Matthew's, since the two lists disagree about the name of Jesus's grandfather and almost every other ancestor. Luke's list includes only two of the kings from the time of the monarchy (perhaps suggesting that Jesus is descended from David through a line of ancestors who were not kings). As well, Luke's genealogy traces the ancestry of Jesus all the way back to Adam, an artistic way of saying that Jesus is savior of all humanity rather than primarily the fulfillment of Jewish hopes.

Again, historical reliability is of secondary importance in the infancy narratives; their primary purpose is to describe the reign of God and the greatness of Jesus, and to persuade the reader to believe the good news on a level much deeper than the search for historical facts.

4. SECTION 1: TWO ANNUNCIATIONS AND THE VISITATION

a) The Role of John the Baptist

Luke weaves accounts of the conception and birth of John the Baptist into his narrative of the conception of Jesus. Though most Christians don't connect JBap to the celebration of Christmas, Luke's gospel did make that connection, and liturgical tradition has honored Luke's insight. The following discussion of the role of JBap in the gospels is inspired in part by the seemingly unusual fact that readings about JBap's ministry (as an adult, setting the stage for Jesus's adult ministry) are part of the liturgy of Advent, the season of preparation for Christmas.

The first question to be considered in this setting is, "What are we celebrating at Christmas?" The obvious, simple answer is, "The birth of Jesus." Still, the centuries-old tradition of the church includes many more factors in the celebration. The word "advent" means "coming"; the focus of the annual celebration of Advent and Christmas is the coming of Jesus in the past (not only at his birth, but also as an adult proclaiming the reign of God), in the present (his coming into human lives to bring wholeness to every generation) and in the future (his expected coming at the end of history—both the history of each individual at personal death, and the history of humanity). This kind of complexity is embedded in Catholic liturgy, but is rarely explained as the church simplifies its proclamation for ordinary worship.

We are reminded about JBap during Advent because he prepared in particular for Jesus's proclamation of the reign of God, not for Jesus's birth. Luke included stories about the childhood of JBap in his infancy narrative for the same purpose—JBap points forward to the pivotal role of the adult Jesus in the story of the salvation of humanity.

In Jewish tradition and in the gospels, there is a strand of thought about JBap that connects him with the prophet Elijah. The source of the tradition is found in 2 Kings 2:11. Elijah leaves the earth and ascends to heaven in a whirlwind, but the narrative does not state that he ever died. A tradition developed that before the Messiah came, Elijah would return to earth to prepare for his coming. Still today at Passover dinners, one place at table is reserved for Elijah; during the rite, the youngest child in the gathering is sent to open the front door of the house and see whether Elijah is coming.

In the gospels, the expectation that Elijah will return to prepare for the Messiah is referred to fairly often. In Mark 8:28, Jesus asks, "Who do people say that I am?" The disciples' first response ("John the Baptist") is puzzling,[23] but they go on to the idea that some people think that Jesus is fulfilling the Elijah role of preparing for the coming of the Messiah. When Jesus asks the disciples what they themselves think, Peter replies that they believe that Jesus is the Messiah, not the forerunner.

The hope that Elijah will return to prepare for the coming of the Messiah is also referred to in John 1:21 when the religious leaders from Jerusalem interrogate JBap about his role. When they ask, "Who are you?" JBap replies, "I am not the Messiah." When they go on to ask whether he is Elijah, JBap is reported to have *denied* that he is filling the role of Elijah returned to prepare the way for the Messiah. In Matthew 11:14, however, Jesus makes the statement, "If you are prepared to believe it, he [JBap] is the Elijah who is to come." Luke refers to the same tradition in 1:17, which will be discussed below.

According to all the gospels, JBap never refers to himself in terms of the return of Elijah, but instead echoes Isaiah 40:3–4 about preparing a way for the Lord in the wilderness. That self-understanding doesn't seem essentially different from the role of Elijah that he is reported to have denied. The Isaiah passage itself deserves an interpretation which would explore its original

23. Does it imply that Jesus's Galilean neighbors have heard of JBap, but have never seen him, and perhaps don't realize that he has been killed?

meaning (related to the return of the Jewish people from exile in Babylon) and its fulfillment meaning as the early Christian community understood it with regard to JBap, but that interpretation will only be mentioned here.

I hope that this background information will help you to understand why Luke included narratives of JBap's birth in the "overture" to his gospel. Every year, the liturgy of Advent reminds us that the adult JBap called everyone to integrity in preparation for Jesus's adult proclamation of the reign of God. Every year, we are invited to renew our dedication to the reign of God and to prepare for Jesus's coming again into our lives at Christmas.

b) The Annunciation to Zechariah

In the days of King Herod of Judea, there was a priest named Zechariah, who belonged to the priestly order of Abijah. His wife was a descendant of Aaron, and her name was Elizabeth. Both of them were righteous before God, living blamelessly according to all the commandments and regulations of the Lord. But they had no children, because Elizabeth was barren, and both were getting on in years. Once when he was serving as priest before God and his section was on duty, he was chosen by lot, according to the custom of the priesthood, to enter the sanctuary of the Lord and offer incense. Now at the time of the incense offering, the whole assembly of the people was praying outside. Then there appeared to him an angel of the Lord, standing at the right side of the altar of incense. When Zechariah saw him, he was terrified; and fear overwhelmed him. But the angel said to him, "Do not be afraid, Zechariah, for your prayer has been heard. Your wife Elizabeth will bear you a son, and you will name him John. You will have joy and gladness, and many will rejoice at his birth, for he will be great in the sight of the Lord. He must never drink wine or strong drink; even before his birth he will be filled with the Holy Spirit. He will turn many of the people of Israel to the Lord their God. *With the spirit and power of Elijah he will go before him, to turn the hearts of parents*

> *to their children, and the disobedient to the wisdom of the*
> *righteous, to make ready a people prepared for the Lord."*
> Zechariah said to the angel, "How will I know that this
> is so? For I am an old man, and my wife is getting on
> in years." The angel replied, "I am Gabriel. I stand in
> the presence of God, and I have been sent to speak to
> you and to bring you this good news. But now, because
> you did not believe my words, which will be fulfilled in
> their time, you will become mute, unable to speak, until
> the day these things occur." Meanwhile the people were
> waiting for Zechariah, and wondered at his delay in the
> sanctuary. When he did come out, he could not speak
> to them, and they realized that he had seen a vision in
> the sanctuary. He kept motioning to them and remained
> unable to speak. When his time of service was ended,
> he went to his home. After those days his wife Elizabeth
> conceived, and for five months she remained in seclu-
> sion. (Luke 1:5–24, emphasis added)

The announcement of the conception of JBap has a few interesting points to be noticed. Recall that "angel" means "messenger,"
and it could be said that the person having the dream or vision
is listening to the voice of God, in whatever way God communi-
cates with humans. The name Zechariah means "God remembers."
(Notice the abbreviated form of the name of God at the end of the
name.)

First, identifying Zechariah as a priest and his wife as a descendant of Aaron establishes JBap as a member of the tribe of
Levi. The high priests who dominated temple worship in Jerusalem were like a royal family who had great political power and who
could pass their position on to their descendants. There were in-
numerable other members of the tribe of Levi[24] who retained their
heritage as belonging to the priestly tribe, but who had to support
their families by other means, since they might be permitted to
perform some temple functions only rarely in their lives. Such is

---

24. Jewish people who trace their heritage to the tribe of Levi are still
identified by their names (given names and surnames including Levine, Levy,
Levin). The Hebrew word for priest is *cohen*, also a current Jewish surname.

the setting of the angel announcement to Zechariah in the temple of Jerusalem.

Second, a miraculous element is reported in the conception of JBap: like many heroes in the Scriptures, he is born of a couple who are past the age of child-bearing. Thus it is understood that God took a direct part in bringing this important religious leader into the world—but Luke is also setting the stage for a *more* miraculous intervention in the conception of Jesus.

Third, Luke 1:15–17 gives a summary of the role of JBap as the later Christian community remembered it. JBap is remembered as an ascetic (Luke 1:16, see also Luke 7:34), in sharp contrast to Jesus who was sometimes criticized for not obeying dietary rules (see Luke 7:35). In verse 17, the mission of JBap is described thus: "With the spirit and power of Elijah he will . . . turn the hearts of parents to their children, and the disobedient to the wisdom of the righteous, to make ready a people prepared for the Lord." Notice the reference to the Elijah tradition that continues in Jewish observances to this day, and to JBap's adult ministry, calling people to integrity in preparation for the Messiah's coming. Later in the gospel, Luke gives extensive treatment to the preaching of JBap (3:1–18) and to Jesus's comments about JBap's work (7:18–35). When you read those passages, consider what JBap might say to us.

According to the story, Zechariah is punished with muteness for asking, "How will I know that this is so? For I am an old man." In the next episode, Mary asks almost the same question ("How can this be, since I am a virgin?" Luke 1:34) but she receives no punishment and is praised for accepting her role as mother of Jesus. To accuse God of inconsistency in reacting differently to the responses of these two characters is to accept the stories at face value as if that is what really happened. Instead, realize that the stories are intended to express the greatness of Jesus and the lesser role of JBap.

c) The Annunciation to Mary

The well-known account of the angel's announcement to Mary is commemorated each year on March 25, nine months before Christmas. Traditional interpretation has focused on the issue of the historical reliability of the virginal conception,[25] but we intend to emphasize the story's expressions about the greatness of Jesus.

In this episode, surprisingly, the angel's central point (as presented by the author) is that Jesus fulfills the Jewish expectation of a great king in the spirit of King David—not the most edifying statement about Jesus's greatness, but apparently one that was important to Luke's Christian community.

> In the sixth month the angel Gabriel was sent by God to a town in Galilee called Nazareth, to a virgin engaged to a man whose name was Joseph, of the house of David. The virgin's name was Mary. And he came to her and said, "Greetings, favored one! The Lord is with you." But she was much perplexed by his words and pondered what sort of greeting this might be. The angel said to her, "Do not be afraid, Mary, for you have found favor with God. And now, you will conceive in your womb and bear a son, and you will name him Jesus. He will be great, and will be called the Son of the Most High, and the Lord God will give to him the throne of his ancestor David. He will reign over the house of Jacob forever, and of his kingdom there will be no end." Mary said to the angel, "How can this be, since I am a virgin?" The angel said to her, "The Holy Spirit will come upon you, and the power of the Most High will overshadow you; therefore the child to be born will be holy; he will be called Son of God. And now, your relative Elizabeth in her old age has also conceived a son; and this is the sixth month for her who was said to be barren. For nothing will be impossible with God." Then Mary said, "Here am I, the servant of the Lord; let

25. Remember that the doctrine of "Immaculate Conception" relates to *Mary*'s being conceived "without the stain of original sin" in her mother's womb. It is celebrated on Dec 8, nine months before the "birthday" of Mary, celebrated on Sept 8.

it be with me according to your word." Then the angel departed from her. (Luke 1:26–38)

... TO A VIRGIN ENGAGED TO A MAN NAMED JOSEPH ...

Luke twice uses the word "virgin" (*parthenos* in Greek) in the opening verses of this episode. The meaning of the word for Luke is clear. The reason for his use of the term is less clear, perhaps to emphasize that Mary was not yet married.

GREETINGS, FAVORED ONE. THE LORD IS WITH YOU ... DO NOT BE AFRAID; YOU HAVE FOUND FAVOR WITH GOD.

Whether we understand that Mary had a vision of a seemingly embodied messenger, or a dream, or a personal spiritual encounter with God, the natural reaction is fear, and the first response from the messenger is reassurance. When we experience the call of God, whether in a blinding flash of insight or a life-changing event, most of us would respond with fear at the changes that are inevitably involved. For too many of us, the result is often that we ignore the challenge and lapse back into our previous more comfortable lifestyle. What recent events in your life could be described as a call from God? How did you respond?

As in Matthew's gospel, Luke's emphasis is on the intervention of God: the child is God's gift, the result of God's action.[26] Luke understands that Mary was favored by God, and that her life was forever changed by this assignment to be the mother of Jesus.

---

26. Notice that Luke, unlike Matthew, does not mention the possibility of adultery as the source of the pregnancy.

You will bear a son and you will name him Jesus

Recall the note on the meaning of the name Jesus in the commentary on Matthew's infancy narrative. Jesus (in Hebrew *Yeho-shua*) means "Yahweh saves."

He will be great and will be called the Son of the Most High

"Son of the Most High" is the first title of honor given to Jesus in Luke, and it has an intriguing history in Hebrew, Roman and Christian contexts.

This relatively unusual title for Jesus ("Son of the Most High") echoes Genesis 14:18–20, very early in God's relationship with the Jewish people. Abraham meets Melchizedek, who is identified as the king of Salem and a priest of "God Most High." Many scholars would identify Melchizedek as a Jebusite, one of the indigenous peoples who lived in the Holy Land before the time of Moses. (Compare the native peoples of North America or Australia before the arrival of Europeans.) Their capital, Salem, later became "Jerusalem." (The name "Salem" is connected to the Hebrew/Arabic word for peace, *shalom/salaam*.) Melchizedek is introduced as the king of Salem and a priest of the Canaanite god known as El Elyon, or "God Most High." Christian interpretation has tended to equate Melchizedek's god with God, but that was not likely the real situation at the root of the story in Genesis. Read the story again with this new background. Melchizedek, the ruler of a settled people, meets the nomad Abraham, and as a gesture of welcome, calls blessings on Abraham in the name of the local god, El Elyon. In the early centuries of their religion, the Israelites were not yet "theoretical monotheists." They worshipped only one God, but they could accept the idea that other people had their own gods. Often the Israelites would claim that their God was the greatest of the gods, the God of gods. Perhaps not until the fourth century BCE did they begin to realize that the gods of their neighbors didn't exist at all: "They have eyes, but they do not see . . ." (Ps 115:4–8).

For later Jews, and clearly for Luke, "God Most High" refers to the one God of Jews and Christians, but there is another implied reference in the use of this title, as well as "Son of God." The Caesars[27] took the title of son of god for themselves. Julius Caesar was praised as divine after his death, and his adopted son who became Caesar Augustus (mentioned in Luke 2:1) called himself *divi filius* (son of the divine one). Luke is written for a Gentile audience, Christians who were trying to survive despite being persecuted within the Empire. When we read "Son of the Most High" or "Son of God" as titles to honor Jesus in Luke, it may be helpful to realize that Luke is presenting Jesus as competition for Caesar. For Luke, Jesus, not Caesar, is the real Son of God.

At the same time, the later Christian understanding of the greatness of Jesus went beyond his being a king from the line of David, and "better than the Caesar." They understood that in the life of Jesus, God was present on earth in a different way than God had ever been on earth before. In the teaching and actions of Jesus, Christians felt that they experienced the presence of God among them, and the best phrase they developed to express that belief was to call Jesus "Son of God."

GOD WILL GIVE HIM THE THRONE OF HIS ANCESTOR DAVID; HE WILL REIGN OVER THE HOUSE OF JACOB FOREVER, AND OF HIS KINGDOM THERE WILL BE NO END

Again, the angel's message is surprisingly limited—it promises that Jesus will be a new David for the Jewish people, the fulfillment of their expectation of a great king who would set the people free of foreign invaders and inaugurate a utopian kingdom of peace.

In the time of Joshua and the Judges as in the days of the monarchy, Yahweh was considered a warrior-God, approving of the killing of people whose only offence was defending their own homelands, exacting retribution for wrongdoing, and helping

---

27. Caesar in Latin (= *Kaiser* in German = *Czar* in Russian) means "emperor."

David to defeat his enemies. The popular hope for Messiah involved achieving peace through victory. Roman leaders had the same goal: the vaunted *pax romana* was achieved by subjugating peoples across a wide radius, combined with the deification of their victorious leaders under titles like savior and son of god.

The followers of Jesus are presented (especially in Mark) as continuing to hope for "peace through victory" under the leadership of a new David. They seem not to have understood Jesus's understanding of the reign of God as bringing "peace through justice."[28]

For more on the "royal theme" of messianic expectation, see below under "Son of God."

"HOW CAN THIS BE, SINCE I KNOW NO MAN?" "THE HOLY SPIRIT WILL COME UPON YOU, AND THE POWER OF THE MOST HIGH WILL OVERSHADOW YOU . . ."

Mary's question and the angel's response have always been understood as Luke's way of expressing his belief that Jesus's life began by the direct action of the Creator in Mary's womb. The essence of that doctrine is that Jesus is God's gift to humanity. Neither the human race nor the Jewish tradition can claim credit for the greatness of Jesus, because Jesus came to us as the result of God's direct action.

If we look at the dialogue at face value, it does not necessarily imply a virgin conception. Mary's question could simply mean, "I'm not fully married yet," and the answer could mean "God will take care of it," implying as Jewish tradition believed, that the power of God's Spirit is involved in the conception of *every* child. One rabbinical saying taught that "three are involved in the birth of every child: the father, the mother, and the Holy Spirit."

Still, in appears that the intention of Luke, especially with his use of the term "virgin" in 1:27, is to assert that the life of Jesus began by a creative act of God in the womb of a virgin.

28. The contrast of "peace through victory" and "peace through justice" is taken from Borg and Crossan, *First Christmas*, 156–67.

THE CHILD . . . WILL BE CALLED SON OF GOD

The title "Son of God" links Jesus to the Jewish expectation of a Messiah-king. The kings of Israel were called sons of God in a way that was different from ordinary believers. The day of a king's coronation (or more properly, anointing) was considered to be the day of his birth as God's son in a special way. Psalm 2 is a coronation psalm in which God is portrayed as warning and mocking the kings of "the nations" (the Gentiles), and declaring that God's king is enthroned in Jerusalem (Zion). In the poem, the king goes on to declare that God said to him at his anointing, "You are my son; I have begotten you today."

In one of the most beautiful and memorable prophecies of Isaiah, the poet imagines himself already living in the utopian kingdom of the Messiah (notice that verbs are in the present perfect tense), rejoicing in a great light, exulting as at the harvest, and free of oppression and war because the new Messiah-king has been crowned.

> The people who walked in darkness have seen a great
> light;
> those who lived in a land of deep darkness—
> on them the light has shined.
> You have multiplied the nation,
> you have increased its joy;
> They rejoice before you as with joy at the harvest,
> as people exult when dividing plunder.
> For the yoke of their burden,
> and the bar across their shoulders,
> the rod of their oppressor,
> you have broken as on the day of Midian.
> For all the boots of the tramping warriors,
> and all the garments rolled in blood
> shall be burned as fuel for the fire.
> For a child has been born for us,
> a son is given to us;
> Authority rests upon his shoulders; . . .
> His authority shall grow continually,
> and there will be endless peace

for the throne of David and his kingdom.
He will establish and uphold it
with justice and with righteousness
from this time onward and forevermore. (Isa 9:2–7)

The image in the ninth-last line is not about the birth of a child; it is about the coronation of a king as Son of God, as the ensuing lines clearly express.

The early Christians remembered the images of Psalm 2 and Isaiah 9 and applied them to Jesus at his baptism, as the voice from heaven proclaims that Jesus is God's beloved son, the fulfillment of the Jewish hope for a messiah-king who would establish an everlasting kingdom of peace. Luke's infancy narrative proclaims that Jesus is God's beloved son, not from the time of his baptism, but from the time of his conception in Mary's womb.

For the gospel writer and his community, writing long after the resurrection, Jesus was Son of God from the beginning of his life, not only as the fulfillment of messianic expectation, not only as competing with the Caesars (who were revered as sons of god), but as embodying the reality of God in a profound way in a single human life. Christians had come to believe that in looking at Jesus, they were seeing God in action, healing people, leading them to wholeness, teaching them what are the true values in human life. As the tradition developed after the gospels were written, that belief about Jesus became part of a doctrine that came to be known as "Trinity," but Luke's theology had not developed that far when the gospel was written.

Here am I, the servant of the Lord

Luke portrays Mary as accepting the assignment given to her by God. All of us are invited to echo her favorable reception of God's invitation, repeatedly during our lives. Like Mary, we are invited to accept the reign of God in our hearts, in the confident belief that God will lead us toward wholeness.

Mary appears only once in the body of Luke's gospel, and it is again in the spirit of obedient acceptance of the word of God.

The single gospel episode is found in Luke 8:19–21, and it offers a fascinating example of how one gospel writer edits another gospel for a deliberate purpose. To explore that passage in Luke, we must consider as background the role of Mary in the Gospel of Mark.

The Gospel of Mark was written more than fifteen years before Luke, with no stories of Jesus's childhood, and was likely used by Luke as a source. Mark 3:20–21 reports that the family of Jesus[29] tried to stop his preaching early in his career because "they" were saying that "he has gone out of his mind," and the common vigilante punishment for mental illness was severe.[30] The Greek verb translated here as "were saying" implies the pronoun "they," and does not specify whether "they" are the people of Nazareth or Jesus's family.

A little later (Mark 3:31–35), when Jesus is surrounded by a crowd inside a house, his mother and his family send a message that they want to talk to him. Knowing that they want him to stop his preaching, Jesus rebuffs them with the scornful line, "Who are my mother and my brothers? . . . Whoever does the

29. All three Synoptic Gospels, even the two that tell of the virgin conception of Jesus, report that Jesus had brothers and sisters. Mark 6:3 and Matthew 13:55–56 give the names of four brothers and refer to plural sisters (see also Luke 8:19–20). John 7:3–10 refers to his brothers as not supporting him. James, the brother of the Lord, is mentioned by Paul as a leader of the Jerusalem community (Gal 1:19). Still, the belief that Mary was "ever virgin" (that she never had sexual intercourse, and had no other children than Jesus) has been a tradition of very long standing in the Catholic Church. The tradition depends on an understanding that the people listed in Mark 6:3 are members of Jesus's extended family, "brethren" who were really cousins or step-siblings rather than blood brothers. On the other hand, the proper Greek word for "cousin" or "relative" was known to the gospel writers, and is used to identify the mother of John the Baptist as Mary's relative (Luke 1:36). The New Testament makes no effort to claim that Jesus was Mary's only child; indeed by giving the names of four brothers and referring to his sisters in the plural, the gospels indicate that Mary bore at least seven children, and was fortunate enough to see them grow to adulthood in a time when childhood mortality was commonplace. (That calculation was stated in *Marginal Jew*, vol. 1, by the respected Catholic priest-scholar John Meier.)

30. See Mark 5:3–5 for a description of contemporary treatment of manic mental illness: the townspeople chained this man to the tombstones near their village.

will of God is my brother and sister and mother." According to Mark (closer to the events, and with no knowledge of an angel announcement to Mary), Jesus's family, including his mother, were not among his disciples during his public ministry, and tried to terminate his ministry because "they" thought he was insane. As well, Mary is not mentioned in a list of women who were present at the crucifixion.[31]

In chapter 8:19–21, Luke has significantly edited the testimony of Mark 3:31–35 to harmonize it with Mary's acceptance in Luke 1:38 ("Here am I, the servant of the Lord"). In reporting that Jesus's mother and brothers came to him but could not reach him because of the crowd, Luke omits the verses that report that Jesus's family tried to stop him from preaching, and also omits the reproach, "Who are my mother and my brothers?" When it is related to Jesus that his mother and brothers want to see him, he simply responds, "My mother and my brothers are those who hear the word of God and do it." When you understand the implications of that saying as Luke reports it, Mary is *included* in the group who "hear the word of God and do it." Her identity as the faithful servant has been established in Luke 1:38, and is not contradicted but affirmed in 8:21.

Mary's life was significantly different from ours so many centuries later, but one major area of life in which she can be a model for all of us is to "hear the word of God and keep it." Consistently in our lives, we need to listen for the invitation of God. To refer again to the gospel theme of the reign of God, we can constantly re-affirm our willingness to open our hearts to the transforming spiritual power of God, both in the life-changing decisions of our lives (like this decision made by Mary), and in our everyday decisions to live in love, wisdom and courage.

31. Only John's gospel reports that Mary was present at the crucifixion. John also, alone among the gospels, reports the scene of the wedding feast at Cana, where Mary intervenes on behalf of the wedding party. Acts of the Apostles 1:14, written by the author of Luke, reports that Mary was with the disciples of Jesus after the resurrection.

d) Mary Visits Her Cousin Elizabeth

The two angel announcement stories (to Zechariah and to Mary) are brought together in the narrative of Mary's visit to her cousin Elizabeth, who lived in the hill country of Judea, perhaps sixty miles from Mary's home, which was in Nazareth according to Luke.

> In those days Mary set out and went with haste to a Judean town in the hill country, where she entered the house of Zechariah and greeted Elizabeth. When Elizabeth heard Mary's greeting, the child leaped in her womb. And Elizabeth was filled with the Holy Spirit and exclaimed with a loud cry, "Blessed are you among women, and blessed is the fruit of your womb. And why has this happened to me, that the mother of my Lord comes to me? For as soon as I heard the sound of your greeting, the child in my womb leaped for joy. And blessed is she who believed that there would be a fulfillment of what was spoken to her by the Lord." And Mary said,
> "My soul magnifies the Lord, and my spirit rejoices in God my Savior,
> for he has looked with favor on the lowliness of his servant.
> Surely, from now on all generations will call me blessed;
> for the Mighty One has done great things for me,
> and holy is his name.
> His mercy is for those who fear him from generation to generation.
> He has shown strength with his arm;
> he has scattered the proud in the thoughts of their hearts.
> He has brought down the powerful from their thrones,
> and lifted up the lowly;
> he has filled the hungry with good things, and sent the rich away empty.
> He has helped his servant Israel, in remembrance of his mercy,
> according to the promise he made to our ancestors,
> to Abraham and to his descendants forever."
> And Mary remained with her about three months and then returned to her home. (Luke 1:39–56)

• *Jesus's Connection to John the Baptist*

The tribal heritage of Mary is never disclosed in the gospels. Joseph is portrayed as belonging to the tribe of Judah, the family of King David, but Mary is here presented as a relative of the wife of a priest. Zechariah belonged to the tribe of Levi. Some commentators suggest that Luke (by mentioning Mary's kinship with the wife of a member of the tribe of Levi) is subtly presenting Jesus as the fulfillment of some Jewish believers' hope for a priestly Messiah as well as a monarch from the tribe of David.

What is more interesting is the suggestion that Jesus and JBap were cousins. Granted, there might be little contact between related families living so far apart, but there is no hint in the gospels that Jesus and JBap knew each other before Jesus heard of JBap's preaching and came south to listen to him and accept baptism from him. ("I myself did not know him," says JBap in John 1:31, 33.) Luke reports that JBap proclaimed that "one who is more powerful than I is coming," (Luke 3:16) but does not say that JBap identified Jesus as "the one who is coming." Though Luke's narrative of the visitation says that JBap "leaped for joy" in his mother's womb at hearing the voice of "the mother of my Lord," later in the gospel Luke reports that John sent messengers to ask Jesus, "Are you the one who is to come, or shall we look for another?" (Luke 7:19) Jesus's response, like most rabbis, is not a clear affirmation, but a command that the messengers tell JBap what they have seen of Jesus's work, and let JBap draw his own conclusion.

Matthew's gospel (but not Luke's) reports that JBap demurs when Jesus asks to be baptized, saying, "I need to be baptized by you" (Matt 3:14). Most commentators feel that this brief remark is the product of the community's uncertainty, fifty years after the resurrection, about Jesus's motivation for being baptized by JBap.

The Gospel of John is almost strident in its repeated insistence that Jesus is far more important than JBap. "He (JBap) himself was not the light, but he came to testify to the light" (John 1:8). JBap says, "You yourselves are my witnesses that I said, 'I am not the Messiah,'... He must increase and I must decrease" (John 3:28,

30). Those are JBap's last words in the Gospel of John; he never speaks again.

The Gospel of John alone reports that JBap does clearly identify Jesus as the expected one, using the now-familiar symbol of "Lamb of God who takes away the sin of the world" (John 1:29–34). "I myself have seen and have testified that this is the Son of God" (John 1:34).

Curiously, though, the Gospel of John also seems to testify that Jesus was a disciple of JBap for a time, and cooperated in the baptism ministry of JBap (see John 3:22–24)—though the same gospel a few verses later denies that Jesus did any baptizing as a disciple of JBap (John 4:1–3).

Nowhere in any gospel, though, except for this visitation story in Luke, is there any indication that Jesus and JBap were related, or that they knew each other before meeting in the course of JBap's ministry.

• *Mary's Canticle of Praise and Thanks*

(*"Magnificat"* is the opening word in the Latin translation of Mary's canticle.)

Commentators agree that Mary's song of praise is not a transcript of what she said to Elizabeth that day; this canticle is a work of art created for theological purposes. Scholars also agree that the poem does not explicitly refer to the coming of the Messiah and really is not specifically Christian, but could easily have been said or written by any devout Jewish or Christian person who felt favored by God. There is uncertainty about the authorship of this and the other three canticles that appear in Luke, but most agree that they were not written by the author himself (they are too Jewish in spirit), but were composed by a Jewish or Jewish-Christian poet. Then they were included by the author to enhance his narrative about the childhood of JBap and Jesus. With that information in mind, any of us can re-read the poem as referring to *ourselves* as God's lowly servant, praising God for doing great things for us.

The central theme of the poem is also central to the teaching of the Jewish prophets and of Jesus: God supports the poor, and will bring down the rich and powerful. In the psalms, the Hebrew word *anawim* is translated as meek, lowly, humble, afflicted: the prophets speak of the *anawim* as the "remnant" who will remain faithful no matter what hardships they or their people must endure. In this canticle, Mary is portrayed as one of the faithful poor. There are groups of contemporary Christians who consider themselves the *anawim* of our time. All of us must ask ourselves whether we want to belong to this remnant of faithful and poor people, because these are the people whom God favors. Too often we prefer comfort to poverty and lowliness.

Throughout this gospel, and more than other gospels, Luke presents Jesus's revolutionary disdain for the rich and powerful; the theme begins in this memorable poem which the author has placed on the lips of Mary.

> God's mercy is for those who fear him . . .
> He has scattered the proud in the thoughts of their hearts.
> He has brought down the powerful from their thrones
> and lifted up the lowly;
> He has filled the hungry with good things,
> and sent the rich away empty.

5. SECTION 2: TWO BIRTHS AND THE PRESENTATION OF JESUS IN THE TEMPLE

a) The Birth and Naming of John the Baptist

> Now the time came for Elizabeth to give birth, and she bore a son. Her neighbors and relatives heard that the Lord had shown his great mercy to her, and they rejoiced with her. On the eighth day they came to circumcise the child, and they were going to name him Zechariah after his father. But his mother said, "No; he is to be called John." They said to her, "None of your relatives has this name." Then they began motioning to his father to find out what name he wanted to give him. He asked for a

writing tablet and wrote, "His name is John." And all of them were amazed. Immediately his mouth was opened and his tongue freed, and he began to speak, praising God. Fear came over all their neighbors, and all these things were talked about throughout the entire hill country of Judea. All who heard them pondered them and said, "What then will this child become?" For, indeed, the hand of the Lord was with him. Then his father Zechariah was filled with the Holy Spirit and spoke this prophecy:

"Blessed be the Lord God of Israel,

for he has looked favorably on his people and redeemed them.

He has raised up a mighty savior for us in the house of his servant David,

as he spoke through the mouth of his holy prophets from of old,

that we would be saved from our enemies and from the hand of all who hate us.

Thus he has shown the mercy promised to our ancestors,

and has remembered his holy covenant,

the oath that he swore to our ancestor Abraham,

to grant us that we, being rescued from the hands of our enemies,

might serve him without fear, in holiness and righteousness before him all our days.

And you, child, will be called the prophet of the Most High;

for you will go before the Lord to prepare his ways,

to give knowledge of salvation to his people by the forgiveness of their sins.

By the tender mercy of our God, the dawn from on high will break upon us,

to give light to those who sit in darkness and in the shadow of death,

to guide our feet into the way of peace."

The child grew and became strong in spirit, and he was in the wilderness until the day he appeared publicly to Israel. (Luke 1:57–80)

As mentioned in the discussion of Matthew's infancy narrative, the meaning of *Yeho-hanan* (John) is "Yahweh is gracious."

Zechariah's beautiful canticle was likely composed by a Christian of Jewish heritage and inserted into Luke's narrative. Although it is presented as being spoken by the father of JBap before the birth of Jesus, it praises God for sending Jesus to be the savior of the world, fulfilling God's promises to Abraham by forgiving people's sins and guiding them into the ways of peace. The echoes of the Jewish tradition in the canticle are mingled with Christian themes that would not likely be spoken by a Jewish priest, before Jesus was born. Try to read the canticle first as a Jewish person would read it, and later as a Christian reader. In both cases, notice the emphasis on the action of God to bring people like us to holiness, righteousness and peace.

b) The Birth and Naming of Jesus

> In those days a decree went out from Emperor Augustus that all the world should be registered. This was the first registration and was taken while Quirinius was governor of Syria. All went to their own towns to be registered. Joseph also went from the town of Nazareth in Galilee to Judea, to the city of David called Bethlehem, because he was descended from the house and family of David. He went to be registered with Mary, to whom he was engaged and who was expecting a child. While they were there, the time came for her to deliver her child. And she gave birth to her firstborn son and wrapped him in bands of cloth, and laid him in a manger, because there was no place for them in the inn. (Luke 2:1–7)

A DECREE WENT OUT FROM THE EMPEROR AUGUSTUS
THAT ALL THE WORLD SHOULD BE REGISTERED . . .
WHILE QUIRINIUS WAS GOVERNOR OF SYRIA

The census with which Luke begins his narrative of the birth of Jesus is based on inaccurate historical information, and should be understood as a literary device of the author, writing many decades after the events he describes. The author knows that Jesus came from Nazareth, but wants to promote the Christian tradition that he was born in Bethlehem like King David, so he creates a scenario to explain both locations. Recall that Matthew, wanting to promote the same Christian tradition, says that Jesus was born in Joseph's home in Bethlehem and moved to Nazareth for fear of lethal opposition in Jerusalem.

Historians agree that censuses were weapons of domination, used to enumerate conquered peoples for purposes of taxation and conscription. They also agree that the Romans never did try to take a census of "the whole world" (presumably meaning the Roman Empire), and never asked people to return to their ancestral hometown to be counted.

Augustus was emperor from 27 BCE to 14 CE, so he certainly was ruling when Jesus was born. Part of Luke's purpose seems to be the claim that even the famous Caesar Augustus was just a puppet used by God in the process of sending Jesus into the world at a destined location.

Quirinius was governor of Syria from 7 to 14 CE, and there is a record of a census proclaimed by him in Syria and Judea early in his reign, but that would have been some ten years after the birth of Jesus. Luke, writing many decades later, must have heard of the census of Quirinius and decided to use it to explain the journey of Joseph and Mary to Bethlehem, but his connection between the census and the birth of Jesus is historically impossible.

Bethlehem was the birthplace of David, who was born into a nomadic family of shepherds, and who because of his exploits rose in popularity until he was chosen by the people as their king after the death of the first Jewish king Saul, near the year 1000 BCE.

Still, (except for Luke's infancy narrative) Bethlehem was never called the "city of David"—only Jerusalem, the capital during his reign, is usually known as David's city.

As we have seen, Matthew's gospel paraphrases a verse from the prophet Micah 5:2, suggesting that from Bethlehem will arise a ruler "whose origin is from of old." No doubt the early Christians read that prophetic verse literally, and felt that they had to claim that Jesus was born in Bethlehem as David was.

She gave birth . . . wrapped him in bands of cloth, and laid him in a manger

According to Luke 2:5, even in the last weeks of Mary's pregnancy she was still only "betrothed" to Joseph, and had not yet entered full marriage with him. Matthew, of course, states that they were married soon after the angel's announcement to Joseph, and long before the birth. Luke's purpose apparently is to emphasize that Mary remained a virgin through the pregnancy (a statement that Matthew makes explicitly in Matt 1:25).

The brief verse that narrates the birth of Jesus (Luke 2:7) has been lovingly imagined and visualized for almost two millennia. Very little can be added to common understanding, except for the following few observations that deal with the story at face value.

The bands of cloth (or "swaddling clothes" in the memorable phrase of the King James Version) aren't a sign of poverty, but of loving care: still today, new babies are wrapped tightly to keep them warm and secure. Wisdom of Solomon 7:4–6 says that Solomon as a baby was wrapped in swaddling cloths as a sign of the humanity he shared with every mortal, despite his royal stature.

In a desert region, herders would find shelter for their flocks in caves in the umber hills. (European/American images of stables built of wood are inaccurate. So are caves that look to be made of granite boulders.) The Church of the Nativity in Bethlehem was built many centuries ago over a cave which was selected to remember the birth of Jesus as the story was narrated by Luke. Present-day tourist guides recognize that there is no way of knowing exactly where Jesus was born, but say of this cave, "This is where we remember his birth."

Perhaps it is more likely that the author of this account had in mind the courtyard of an inn where tenants could house their animals safely and conveniently. The story could imply that the child was born in such a courtyard, because the rooms in the inn were all occupied. By the way, note that the word "stable" doesn't appear in Luke's narrative.

The manger would likely have been a flat stone with a shallow cavity in which food for the animals would be placed. Some scholars think that placing Jesus in a manger may be an implied reference to Eucharist, whereby Jesus comes to us as food for our inner lives.

Honestly, birthdays (and even birth years, as we can see from the vagueness of datelines about Jesus's birth) were not remembered in ancient times. The date of Christmas was chosen in the fourth century, likely to compete with Roman festivals connected with the winter solstice, after which the days begin to lengthen. In the late third century, the Roman feast of *sol invictus*, the unconquerable sun, was initiated to celebrate the annual rebirth of the sun as it began again to prevail over darkness. In the same season, Christians developed their own more sober celebration of the birth of the Son of God, as "the light of the world." Other aspects of our Christmas festival were added from non-Christian winter festivals of more northern peoples, like the Yule log and the evergreen tree (whose enduring greenness was seen as a sign of everlasting hope).

• *Shepherds and Angels*

> In that region there were shepherds living in the fields, keeping watch over their flock by night. Then an angel of the Lord stood before them, and the glory of the Lord shone around them, and they were terrified. But the angel said to them, "Do not be afraid; for see—I am bringing you good news of great joy for all the people: to you is born this day in the city of David a Savior, who is the Messiah, the Lord. This will be a sign for you: you

> will find a child wrapped in bands of cloth and lying
> in a manger." And suddenly there was with the angel a
> multitude of the heavenly host, praising God and saying,
> "Glory to God in the highest heaven, and on earth peace
> among those whom he favors!" (Luke 2:8–14)

The memorable episode about the shepherds continues the theme of "who accepts Jesus, and what do they do as a result?"— the question that all of us must answer in our own way. Consistent with one of Luke's themes, the people who first welcome Jesus are from the lowest level of society.[32] At the same time, shepherds also evoke the memory of King David, who was never a prince, but began life as a shepherd until he rose to fame because of his exploits in battle, and eventually was chosen by the people to be their king when their first king, Saul, was killed. (By the time John's gospel was written some years after Luke, Jesus himself had come to be identified as "the good shepherd.")

Especially in Luke, Jesus constantly supported poor and "unimportant" people (like the shepherds). No doubt each of us feels some kinship with the shepherds, since all of us feel unappreciated in some ways. Like the shepherds we are called to be open to the good news, whatever radical changes that recognition may impose on our lifestyle.

The announcement comes to the shepherds from a single messenger from God, "and the glory of the Lord shone around them." In the Hebrew Scriptures, the "glory" is the visible presence of God, for example, as God was perceived in a pillar of cloud by day and a pillar of fire by night (Exod 13:21). Luke's account implies that the shepherds are hearing a message from God.

---

32. The *Jewish Annotated New Testament* disputes the common Christian interpretation that shepherds were outcasts from Jewish society.

"To you is born this day in the city of David a Savior who is the Messiah, the Lord."

In the brief proclamation of the angel, Luke has written what amounts to an early Christian creed, proclaiming Jesus as Savior, Messiah and Lord.

The angel's announcement to the shepherds first proclaims that Jesus is our *Savior*. The saving action of God throughout the Scriptures (and into the present) took many forms: God set people free from oppression (both as a community and as individuals); God entered a covenant with people, giving them a sense that singly and together they *belong* to God; alone among the deities of the time, God offered love to people, and invited humans to love God in return; God taught people how to live as worthy members of God's family, and forgave people's failings. All are ways in which God reaches into human lives and leads us to wholeness. That is the meaning of "salvation." The name of Jesus means "God saves"; the life of Jesus was understood as a further example of God's saving action in the world. (Note that there is no reference to "atonement for original sin" in this summary of the meaning of "savior.")

Messiah (or Christ) meant the fulfillment of Jewish hopes. The primary theme in Jewish expectation was for a wise and faithful king to set the people free from oppression and to establish an enduring kingdom of peace. Luke proclaims that Jesus was the fulfillment of that expectation, though he did not seek political leadership as a king.

Lord (*adonai* in Hebrew; *kyrios* in Greek) was the title that Jews used for God from early in their history. Like the Italian word *signore*, lord can be used for any (male) human with authority or power; when people addressed Jesus as "lord" during his lifetime, it would have been with the respect and reverence that disciples express toward their masters. As the decades wore on, Christians began to use the title "Lord" for Jesus in an enhanced way, realizing that it expressed his unique association with God, who had been known as "the Lord."

"To you is born this day in the city of David a Savior who is the Messiah, the Lord" (Luke 2:11). In that very short sentence, likely a form of early Christian creed presented as having been spoken by the angel to the shepherds, Luke has summarized what his early Christian community believed about Jesus and about what Jesus does for us.

THE ANGELS' CANTICLE: "GLORY TO GOD . . . AND ON EARTH PEACE AMONG THOSE GOD FAVORS."

Suddenly the single herald is joined by a choir of angels, whose canticle praises God's continuing initiative to bring wholeness to humanity. The angels' hymn has been immortalized as the opening verse of the Gloria in the Catholic Mass. Its closing phrase emphasizes that it is the action of God that brings peace on earth. It is now agreed that the fourth-century Latin translation of the New Testament erred in writing "peace on earth to people of good will,"[33] a formulation which focuses on the role of *people* in bringing peace by their good will. The current translation reads, "On earth peace among those God favors." It seems like such a tiny change, and yet the Latin expresses exactly the opposite of Luke's intention, which was to emphasize the saving action of *God* in bringing peace by sending Jesus into the world. Regrettably, the Vatican's 2011 revised translation of the prayers of the Mass perpetuates the Latin error.

THE SHEPHERDS' RESPONSE

> When the angels had left them and gone into heaven, the shepherds said to one another, "Let us go now to Bethlehem and see this thing that has taken place, which the Lord has made known to us." So they went with haste and found Mary and Joseph, and the child lying in the manger. When they saw this, they made known what

33. *Et in terra pax hominibus bonae voluntatis.*

had been told them about this child; and all who heard it were amazed at what the shepherds told them. But Mary treasured all these words and pondered them in her heart. The shepherds returned, glorifying and praising God for all they had heard and seen, as it had been told them. (Luke 2:15–20)

Since we are invited to join the shepherds in welcoming the good news, we are also inspired to imitate their response: they hurry to witness the child in the manger, amaze their hearers by reporting their experience, and then go back to their daily lives glorifying and praising God—as do we, praising God daily by noticeably living in a spirit of peace and love.

c) The Presentation of the Child in the Temple[34]

After eight days had passed, it was time to circumcise the child; and he was called Jesus, the name given by the angel before he was conceived in the womb. When the time came for their purification according to the law of Moses, they brought him up to Jerusalem to present him to the Lord (as it is written in the law of the Lord, "Every firstborn male shall be designated as holy to the Lord"), and they offered a sacrifice according to what is stated in the law of the Lord, "a pair of turtledoves or two young pigeons." (Luke 2:21–24)

34. In Jesus's time, there was only one temple in Judaism. It was in Jerusalem. Jews who lived elsewhere in Palestine and around the Mediterranean worshipped at *synagogues* presided over by rabbis. Only in Jerusalem was there a temple where priests of the tribe of Levi offered sacrifices on an altar and presided over the major festivals. The original temple, built by King Solomon, was destroyed by the Babylonians in 586 BCE. A second temple was constructed soon after the return from exile; Herod the Great undertook a major reconstruction of the second temple, which had not been completed by the time of Jesus's death. That temple was destroyed by the Romans in 70 CE. It has never been rebuilt; the site is now occupied by a Muslim mosque and shrine. Modern synagogues that use "temple" in their name contribute to confusion about the difference between the temple and synagogues.

The practice of circumcising newborn male children continues as an initiation rite in Judaism to this day.

Scholars agree that in the subsequent part of this passage that refers to bringing the child to the temple, Luke has confused two separate Jewish rites surrounding childbirth: the redemption of a firstborn male child and the purification of the mother after giving birth. Most likely the author, not having been Jewish, has mistakenly blended these two traditional rituals. The error is of little importance, but the details are as follows:

In the law of Moses[35] firstborn males are considered consecrated to God, and can be "bought back" by the family by the payment of five shekels to the temple treasury. There is no obligation to bring the child to the temple for this procedure.

Elsewhere in the Bible,[36] the mother (Luke seems to think the law refers to both parents) is expected to come to the temple after forty days to be purified of the ritual uncleanness associated with giving birth. That ceremony involves the gift of a lamb or two young pigeons or doves.

The focus in this episode, however, is not the rituals but the prophecies of the elderly righteous Jews who meet the family at the temple.[37]

NOW YOU ARE DISMISSING YOUR SERVANT IN PEACE
. . . A LIGHT FOR REVELATION TO THE GENTILES . . . A
SIGN THAT WILL BE OPPOSED . . .

> Now there was a man in Jerusalem whose name was
> Simeon; this man was righteous and devout, looking

---

35. Exod 13:1, 13:11ff.; Num 8:15–16.

36. Lev 12:6–8.

37. Worth repeating is the contrast between Matthew and Luke with regard to the city of Jerusalem. In Matthew, the entire city is upset at the possibility of the birth of a new king, and the family has to flee to Egypt to escape the violence ordered by the Jerusalem authorities. In Luke, there is no sign of turmoil related to Jerusalem; the family visits the temple in this episode and again twelve years later.

forward to the consolation of Israel, and the Holy Spirit rested on him. It had been revealed to him by the Holy Spirit that he would not see death before he had seen the Lord's Messiah. Guided by the Spirit, Simeon came into the temple; and when the parents brought in the child Jesus, to do for him what was customary under the law, Simeon took him in his arms and praised God, saying,

"Master, now you are dismissing your servant in peace, according to your word;
for my eyes have seen your salvation,
which you have prepared in the presence of all peoples,
a light for revelation to the Gentiles and for glory to your people Israel."

And the child's father and mother were amazed at what was being said about him. Then Simeon blessed them and said to his mother Mary, "This child is destined for the falling and the rising of many in Israel, and to be a sign that will be opposed so that the inner thoughts of many will be revealed—and a sword will pierce your own soul too."

There was also a prophet, Anna the daughter of Phanuel, of the tribe of Asher. She was of a great age, having lived with her husband seven years after her marriage, then as a widow to the age of eighty-four. She never left the temple but worshiped there with fasting and prayer night and day. At that moment she came, and began to praise God and to speak about the child to all who were looking for the redemption of Jerusalem. (Luke 2:25–38)

The poem spoken by Simeon deals with common human themes of separation and death: the devout elderly man has been promised that he will live to see the Messiah; taking the child Jesus in his arms, he announces that he is ready to die in peace. To find a place for ourselves in this scene, some believers might ask themselves how they would change their lives if they knew that death was imminent: is there some good news you hope to hear before you die? Is there something you should say to someone, that you would regret not having said if death separated you? If you would change some aspect of your life if death were imminent, why not make the change immediately?

The last phrases of the poem raise a theme that is very important to Luke: this child is a gift not only to the people of Israel, but is also "a light for revelation to the Gentiles." Whenever "the nations" appears in the Hebrew Scriptures, be sure to notice the word: usually the nations are cast as the enemies of God's people, and terrible fates are invoked upon them. Often, Jewish literature recognizes that the Gentiles are God's children too, and hope is expressed that the salvation of God will extend beyond the Jewish people to "the nations." Members of Luke's community were primarily Gentile Christians; this line of Simeon's poem is intended to support their faith.

Simeon pronounces a further oracle directed to Mary, predicting that the ministry of Jesus will cause division within the Jewish community. All the gospels, and both infancy narratives, dwell on the themes of acceptance and rejection of God's offer. Later in the gospel, Jesus himself is quoted as saying that his radical message is expected to cause division, even within families.

> Do you think that I have come to bring peace to the earth?
> No, I tell you, but rather division!
> From now on, five in one household will be divided
> . . .
> Father against son and son against father . . . (Luke 12:51–53)[38]

Part of the purpose of Advent and Christmas is sincere soul-searching among us who claim to accept the gospel, like the poor shepherds and the aged Simeon and Anna in Luke, or the open-minded magi in Matthew who left behind their comfortable homelands to seek unexpected truth. Our actions reveal our priorities far more clearly that what we say we believe: there is no better season than Advent to explore the priorities that are expressed in our way of life.

38. See also Matt 10:34–35.

One small addendum in response to anticipated questions: Luke 2:33 speaks of Joseph and Mary as the child's mother and father. Commentators speculate that this brief episode was among materials written previously by someone who was not familiar with belief in the virgin conception. It was included in the gospel by the author, who apparently felt no obligation to revise it to be consistent with the account of the annunciation to Mary.

6. CONCLUDING EPISODE: THE YOUNG MAN IN THE TEMPLE

> When they had finished everything required by the law of the Lord, they returned to Galilee, to their own town of Nazareth. The child grew and became strong, filled with wisdom; and the favor of God was upon him. Now every year his parents went to Jerusalem for the festival of the Passover. And when he was twelve years old, they went up as usual for the festival. When the festival was ended and they started to return, the boy Jesus stayed behind in Jerusalem, but his parents did not know it. Assuming that he was in the group of travelers, they went a day's journey. Then they started to look for him among their relatives and friends. When they did not find him, they returned to Jerusalem to search for him. After three days they found him in the temple, sitting among the teachers, listening to them and asking them questions. And all who heard him were amazed at his understanding and his answers. When his parents saw him they were astonished; and his mother said to him, "Child, why have you treated us like this? Look, your father and I have been searching for you in great anxiety." He said to them, "Why were you searching for me? Did you not know that I must be in my Father's house?" But they did not understand what he said to them. Then he went down with them and came to Nazareth, and was obedient to them. His mother treasured all these things in her heart. And Jesus increased in wisdom and in years, and in divine and human favor. (Luke 2:39–52)

In Bible times, people went from childhood to adulthood without intervening stages now known as adolescence or teenage years. Before puberty, children, while treasured, had few of the rights that we now consider essential. They were used as laborers as soon as they were able to help their fathers or mothers; they were not bound by the law of Moses until they became adults (at puberty). Partly because of high mortality rates for children and mothers, and perhaps also because the behavior of sexually-mature young people was difficult to control even by punitive social laws, the age of puberty was the beginning of adulthood and led to marriage promptly, especially for females.

Such is the social setting for the well-known story of Jesus being brought to the temple in Jerusalem at the age of twelve (not quite the age of adulthood for males).

Familiar questions are asked about this episode, usually with the unspoken assumption that it gives a reliable account of an event in Jesus's life. How could parents be so negligent in setting out and travelling a day without realizing that their son was missing? Why was Jesus so rude in responding to his parents' anxious inquiry? If Mary had been told about his identity by an angel, why were his parents astonished at him, and why didn't they understand his response? And, "Surely we must know something more about Jesus's life between infancy and the beginning of his ministry?"

Rationales have been developed to answer each question, but the fundamental answer is that for some fifty years after his resurrection, and eighty years after Jesus's birth, Christians knew nothing at all about his life before his baptism by JBap, except that he was a construction worker from the small Galilean town of Nazareth. The Gospel of Mark begins with the adult ministry of JBap. The narratives we have been studying about Jesus's childhood may have some historical basis (for example, dating his birth in the reigns of King Herod and Augustus Caesar), but they were written primarily for theological purposes rather than for historical reliability. Some of the questions listed above may indicate that this story was written by an independent author who did not know of the story of the angel's annunciation to Mary, and was inserted into the gospel alongside material from other sources without the historical precision that we have come to demand in recent centuries.

This episode, like similar ones in the childhood stories of more ancient scriptural heroes, was written to proclaim that from the beginning of his life, Jesus was destined by God to do great things. It is a story about the young Jesus's intimations of future prominence. Read carefully, the story doesn't make exaggerated claims about Jesus, just that he was listening to the teachers and asking them questions, and that he amazed his hearers with his understanding and his questions. It does indicate that Jesus was fully in touch with his Jewish heritage.

The three days when Jesus was "lost" can be understood as a symbolic prelude to the three days between his death and resurrection: again, the infancy narratives are an introduction to and a summary of what will happen in the body of the gospel. It is always helpful to remember that every statement in every gospel is written in the light of decades of belief that Jesus has conquered death and given it new meaning by rising to new life after his crucifixion.

Jesus's response to his anxious parents should not be understood to portray him as insensitive or impolite. Rather, the author is consciously presenting Jesus as making a "declaration of independence" from his family, on the principle that the requirements of God come before the demands of family.

Luke ends his infancy narrative with a statement that Jesus retreated into anonymity for almost a lifetime as a member of a normal Jewish working family. As the overture to the gospel has indicated, however, he will go beyond his heritage and his family of origin, burst the bonds of tradition and proclaim God's saving intervention to the whole of humanity.

The stage is set. The public ministry of Jesus is about to begin.

Summary
Gospel Overtures

THE GOSPEL ACCORDING TO MATTHEW

The infancy narrative in Matthew's gospel presents Jesus as God's greatest gift to humanity, fulfilling Jewish hopes for a leader like David, following in the footsteps of the patriarch Joseph who escaped death by being brought to Egypt, then coming forth from Egypt like the Israelites under Moses. In his genealogy, Matthew emphasizes that God has made use of female ingenuity and human frailty in guiding the centuries-long process that led to the coming of Jesus, who will save the people from their sins. The people who reject God's gift are the rich and powerful; those who accept Jesus are open-minded people like Joseph and the magi, who are willing to make changes in their traditional lives and embark on an unexpected voyage of discovery.

The body of Matthew's gospel continues the themes that are expressed in the prelude. To summarize excessively, Matthew presents Jesus as the new Moses proclaiming the reign of God, and announcing a new Law (or better, a gospel instead of the law of Moses) in part by means of a proclamation from a new mountain. The gospel recognizes that Jesus will be the cause of division within the community. Jesus will be accepted by some (the poor and the open-minded) and rejected by others (the powerful, the hidebound). All Jesus's teachings and his actions, including his death and resurrection, show us that the true meaning of human life is to be found in openness to God's reign, enabling humans to live with wisdom, courage, self-giving love, and integrity.

Like Mark's community, Matthew's church perceived that God was present and visible in the life of Jesus in a way that God had never previously been present in the world. Well before Jesus's death (the moment of recognition in Mark), Matthew inserts Peter's proclamation, "You are the Christ, the Son of the living God" (Matt 16:18), to express the faith of the community about the twin roles of Jesus which were forecast in the Christmas story—Jesus is Messiah (fulfillment of Jewish hopes) and Son of God.

The theme that Jesus is "God with us" is brought to a memorable conclusion in the last lines of the gospel, when Jesus announces, "I am with you always, to the end of the age" (Matt 28:20).

THE GOSPEL ACCORDING TO LUKE

Luke's gospel arose in a community that was part of the Gentile Roman Empire rather than predominantly of Jewish heritage. Still, Luke's infancy narrative gives great reverence to Jesus's Jewish heritage: his connection to JBap is a major component of the account; Jesus is presented as the fulfillment of Jewish hopes for a great king in the spirit of David; the canticles that are sprinkled through the Christmas stories are all based in the Jewish tradition; the infancy narrative and indeed the entire two-volume work including the gospel and the Acts of the Apostles are centered on the city of Jerusalem.

References to the Gentile world are also found in the infancy narrative: the emperor Augustus is portrayed as being used by God to arrange for the child to be born in Bethlehem, as King David had been; Jesus is proclaimed as Son of God and Savior in defiance of the Romans' giving those titles to their dead emperors; the aged prophet Simeon describes Jesus as "a light for revelation to the Gentiles."

Other themes in the Gospel of Luke that are begun in the infancy narrative include:

- the role of the Holy Spirit, whose overshadowing power brings about the birth of the child, and whose guidance is constantly invoked by Jesus during his ministry;

- respect for women in the overture (Mary, Elizabeth, Anna) and in the gospel (Mary Magdalene, his friends Mary and Martha, the unnamed woman who anointed Jesus's feet and was forgiven, the women of Jerusalem, the women who stayed with Jesus until his death and then prepared his body for burial, and women who were healed or were characters in the parables);

- strong endorsement of the poor and harsh sayings against the rich in both the infancy narratives (the shepherds; Mary's canticle proclaiming that God exalts the lowly and brings down the rich) and the body of the gospel. (In sayings about wealth that are reported in more than one gospel, Luke's version of the teaching is almost always much more radical and challenging.)

Thus both Matthew's and Luke's narratives about Jesus's birth and childhood, as uncertain as they may be on the level of historical fact, provide profound introductions to the theology and themes of those gospels. For the gospels, Christmas celebrates the coming of Jesus into our lives, proclaiming the reign of God, offering spiritual strength, and leading us to wholeness.

Bibliography

Borg, Marcus J. *Jesus: Uncovering the Life, Teachings, and Relevance of a Religious Revolutionary*. New York: HarperCollins, 2006.

Borg, Marcus J., and John Dominic Crossan. *The First Christmas: What the Gospels Really Teach about Jesus's Birth*. New York: HarperOne, 2007.

Cooper, Noel. *Language of the Heart: How to Read the Bible*. Ottawa: Novalis, 2003.

Cooper, Noel. *What Makes Us Whole: Finding God in Contemporary Life*. Collegeville: Liturgical, 2009.

Brown, Raymond E. *The Birth of the Messiah: A Commentary on the Infancy Narratives in Matthew and Luke*. New York: Doubleday, 1978.

Brown, Raymond E. *An Adult Christ at Christmas: Essay on the Three Biblical Christmas Stories*. Collegeville: Liturgical, 1977.

Kelly, Joseph F. *The Birth of Jesus according to the Gospels*. Collegeville: Liturgical, 2008.

Levine, Amy-Jill, and Marc Zvi Brettler, eds. *The Jewish Annotated New Testament*. New York: Oxford University Press, 2011.

Lyonnet, Stanislas, and Léopold Sabourin. *Sin, Redemption and Sacrifice: A Biblical and Patristic Study*. Analecta Biblica 48. Rome: Biblical Institute, 1970.

Meier, John. *A Marginal Jew: Rethinking the Historical Jesus*. Vol. 1. New York: Doubleday, 1991.

Spong, John Shelby. *A New Christianity for a New World*. Online collection of essays, articles and resources. Subscription available at: JohnShelbySpong.com.